M000121795

PLAY BETTER GUITAR IN TEN MINUTES A DAY

PLAY
BETTER
GUITAR IN
TEN
MINUTES
A DAY

PHIL CAPONE

APPLE

A QUARTO BOOK

First published in the UK in
2014 by Apple Press
74–77 White Lion Street
London N1 9PF
UK

www.apple-press.com

Copyright © 2014 Quarto
Publishing plc

All rights reserved. No part
of this publication may be
reproduced, stored in a
retrieval system or transmitted
in any form or by any means,
electronic, mechanical,
photocopying, recording
or otherwise, without the prior
written permission of the
publisher and copyright holder.

ISBN: 978-1-84543-533-2

QUAR:DGWB

Conceived, designed and
produced by
Quarto Publishing plc
The Old Brewery
6 Blundell Street
London N7 9BH

Project editor: Lily de Gatacre
Designer: Elizabeth Healey
Design assistant: Kate Bramley
Photographer: Martin Norris
Proofreader: Claudia Martin
Indexer: Helen Snaith
Art director: Caroline Guest

Creative director: Moira Clinch
Publisher: Paul Carslake

Colour separation in Hong Kong
by Cypress Colours (HK) Ltd.
Printed in China by Midas
Printing Interntional Limited

Contents

About this Book

The Exercises (pages 14–87)

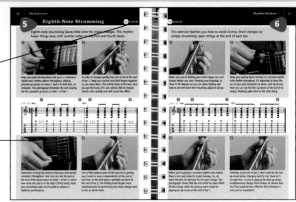

When you see this icon, listen to the track number listed on the CD at the back of the book to hear the exercise played for you.

Clear step-by-step photographs link to specific parts of the notation. They illustrate picking- and fretting-hand positions and highlight tricky spots to look out for within each short exercise.

We begin with 63 self-contained exercises that cover the main areas of guitar-playing technique. The combination of photographs, written instructions and notation will have you playing like a pro in no time.

The Workouts (pages 88–113)

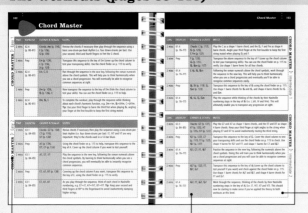

In this section you'll find 48 workouts that will help you to tailor and focus your practice sessions and take your playing to a new level. Each workout is a collection of short exercises adding up to 10 minutes that has been developed to focus on a particular area of guitar playing.

Every skill section contains easy, intermediate and pro workouts so you can continue to challenge yourself as your skills improve.

Relevant scales and chords are cross-referenced – you can find the scale and chord libraries on pages 114–223.

Helpful notes from the author guide you through your workout and offer advice and top tips.

Chord Library (pages 114–149)

An indispensable directory of chords, including seventh, dominant, diminished, half-diminished and power chords, helps you expand your chord vocabulary. See page 114 for further notes on the information included in this section. There is a useful chord finder on page 115.

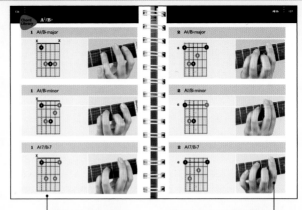

All the details of the chord, including the root note and fingering, are shown diagrammatically.

Photographs help explain the correct fingering and allow you to check your chord shape looks right.

Scale Library (pages 150–223)

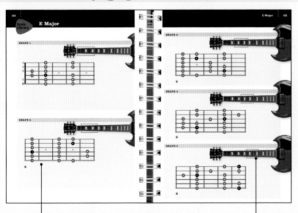

This extensive scale library covering major, minor, pentatonic and harmonic scales is an essential resource for any guitarist. See page 151 for notation guides to help you read the diagrams, and the crucial mode finder.

Easy-to-read colour-coded diagrams make it simple to locate the root notes and get your fingering right.

A red 'locator' box shows you exactly where on the guitar neck the shape is positioned.

The Fingerboard

Finding notes on the fingerboard isn't easy; even accomplished players can be sketchy on this knowledge if they've learnt primarily 'by ear'. This easy-to-use diagram will help you locate any note – and fast! Remember that after the twelfth fret the entire fingerboard repeats an octave higher (starting with the open string note name).

FRET 1
6 – F
5 – A#/B♭
4 – D#/E♭
3 – G#/A♭
2 – C
1 – F

FRET 2
6 – F#/G♭
5 – B
4 – E
3 – A
2 – C#
1 – F#/G♭

FRET 7
6 – B
5 – E
4 – A
3 – D
2 – F#
1 – B

FRET 8
6 – C
5 – F
4 – A#/B♭
3 – D#/E♭
2 – G
1 – C

Fingerboard Repetition
The twelfth fret is the same as the open strings – from then on the notes repeat. For example, fret 13 is the same as fret 1.

23 22 21 20 19 18 17 16 15 14 13 12 1

FRET 3	FRET 4	FRET 5	FRET 6
6 – G	6 – G#/Ab	6 – A	6 – A#/Bb
5 – C	5 – C#/Db	5 – D	5 – D#/Eb
4 – F	4 – F#/Gb	4 – G	4 – G#/Ab
3 – A#/Bb	3 – B	3 – C	3 – C#/Db
2 – D	2 – D#/Eb	2 – E	2 – F
1 – G	1 – G#/Ab	1 – A	1 – A#/Bb

FRET 9	FRET 10	FRET 11	FRET 12
6 – C#/Db	6 – D	6 – D#/Eb	6 – E
5 – F#/Gb	5 – G	5 – G#/Ab	5 – A
4 – B	4 – C	4 – C#/Db	4 – D
3 – E	3 – F	3 – F#/Gb	3 – G
2 – G#/Ab	2 – A	2 – A#/Bb	2 – B
1 – C#/Db	1 – D	1 – D#/Eb	1 – E

Open Strings and Barre Chords

When a string is included in a chord without being fretted, it is called an 'open string', indicated on the chord diagram by an 'O'. Strings not included at all are called out with an 'X'. Where two notes are joined by a bracket on the diagram, a barre chord should be played. See page 114 for more information.

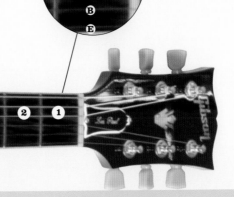

Reading the Dots

Every exercise in this book has been annotated using conventional notation (what musos call 'the dots') and TAB (short for 'tablature').

The majority of guitar publications use this system, so you're probably already comfortable with it. If you're not, don't worry: this short lesson will explain everything you need to know. While it's not necessary to be able to read conventional notation to get the most from this book, you'll find a little time spent now on understanding the basics will be well worth it. Conventional notation is extremely useful in two areas: 1) for describing rhythmic content and 2) for adding fretting-hand fingerings. None of this important information can be conveyed when using TAB alone.

The traditional five-line stave is not guitar specific; it can be used for any musical instrument that reads from the treble clef (some instruments read from different clefs that then change the range of notes on the stave). Each line and space has a corresponding letter name representing a specific pitch, as above.

In this example, you can see how the six lines of the TAB stave represent the six strings of the guitar, starting with the lowest (E) at the bottom. To read TAB all you have to do is convert the number on the line to a fret on the corresponding string – easy!

Here, a stave of conventional notation has been added above the TAB stave. You can see how easy it is to find the notes from the first example when the conventional notation has a stave of TAB added below it.

Here you can see how the notes written in conventional notation describe duration (i.e. rhythm) as well as pitch.

With a little practice you'll soon be able to identify rhythms by sight.

whole note =
4 beats   half note =
2 beats   quarter note =
1 beat   eighth note =
½ beat   16th note =
¼ beat

For each of the notes opposite there's an equivalent rest,
as you can see above. Don't forget: it's not what you
play but what you leave out that counts.

Tuning

**An out-of-tune guitar will make you sound
bad, so it's well worth taking time to learn
how to tune efficiently.**

*Track 1 To help you get in tune,
we've included some tuning notes
on the accompanying CD – each
string is played three times, starting
with the first (high E) string.*

All too often guitar students overlook their tuning,
but playing an out-of-tune guitar not only makes
whatever you play sound terrible, it will also inhibit
your aural skills (developing a good 'ear' is essential
to being a good musician) and could even damage
your guitar. Guitar strings are under a lot of stress,
so even a top-quality instrument won't stay in tune
for long. Check your tuning every time you pick up
your guitar.

Tuning by Ear
This method is called 'relative tuning' since it only
verifies that the guitar is in tune with itself (as
opposed to being in concert pitch). The TAB below
shows you how you can check each pair of strings to
make sure they're nicely in tune. Each pair of notes
produces the same pitch as indicated above the
TAB, so play the strings simultaneously for the best
results. When the strings are nearly in tune, you will

hear a beating or pulsating effect caused by the
slight difference in pitch. As the pitches get closer,
the beating slows, and will disappear altogether
when the strings are completely in tune.

Using a Tuner
An electronic tuner will keep your guitar in concert
pitch. This is important for playing with other
musicians and avoids putting too much (or too little)
stress on the guitar's neck, which can cause it to
bend out of shape. The tuner will indicate whether
the string is in tune, sharp or flat, so all you have to
do is adjust the appropriate machine head (tuning
peg). If your guitar is a long way out of tune, an
electric tuner may not be able to identify the pitch of
the string correctly. If this happens, don't be afraid to
ask your local music shop for help.

1) A   2) D   3) G   4) B   5) E

Picking-Hand Position

The problem with teaching any contemporary guitar style is that there is no right or wrong way to play.

Contemporary guitar playing is all about individuality; it's about creating your own sound. Many of the pioneers were completely self-taught. It is often their unorthodox approach to the instrument that makes them unique. Unfortunately, many teachers are dogmatic about picking technique. This is wrong, because while they may have discovered a system that works for themselves, it won't necessarily work for you. Why spend ages developing the optimum shred-metal picking technique, when all you want to do is play the blues? The following picking-hand positions are intended to provide versatile, non-genre-specific techniques that will allow your playing skills to grow unhindered by bad habits.

Holding the pick

Grasp the pick between your thumb and first finger. Notice how little of the pick remains visible and how it protrudes at a right angle to the thumb – the more of the pick you hold, the easier it is to control.

Picking-hand position for fingerpicking

When fingerpicking, your hand should be suspended above the strings with your thumb remaining parallel to the bass strings. If you keep your fingers in a claw-like shape, you will be able to pick the strings without moving your hand.

Picking-hand position using a pick

Try 'anchoring' the picking hand by gently resting your third and fourth fingers on the scratchplate (these fingers should be loosely held in position so they are free to move as you pick across the strings).

Tip: Don't be afraid to experiment with different types and thicknesses of pick – you may find some more comfortable than others. For fingerstyle playing, try using a thumb pick.

Learn to develop a smooth technique that will allow you to fret notes with the minimum of effort and maximum economy of movement.

Contemporary guitarists can learn a lot from their classically trained cousins, whose art form has evolved over a long period. The fretting-hand technique of classical guitarists has been perfected over hundreds of years. One thing is certain – if you don't make a conscious effort to develop a good fretting-hand technique, you'll join the thousands of guitarists who have had to relearn this technique in order to reach the next level. A professional guitarist can make playing look easy and effortless; this is not because they have a special gift, but because they have spent years perfecting their technique.

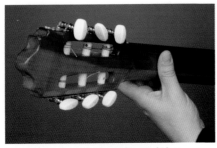

Fretting-hand thumb position
It's important to keep your thumb behind the guitar neck. Some players will occasionally use their thumb to fret notes on the sixth string, but keeping it in this position permanently will put unnecessary strain on your fretting hand.

Keeping close to the fingerboard
By keeping your fingers hovering above the strings, you will be able to fret notes more easily as less finger movement will be required (you will find it hard to do this with your little finger at first).

Angling your fingers
Make sure the tip of each finger approaches the fingerboard directly from above and at a 90-degree angle (to avoid damping adjacent strings). It's also important to fret the note close to the fret to avoid weak and buzzy notes.

Tip: Try to keep your fretting-hand thumb pointing upwards at the back of the guitar neck and your fingers hovering over the strings.

Chapter 1

The Exercises

Directional symbols

You will see directional symbols just above the TAB stave.
A square symbol indicates down-picks and an arrow indicates up-picks.
The same symbols denote down-strums and up-strums.

⊓   down-pick or down-strum

V   up-pick or up-strum

Picking-hand finger symbols

Abbreviations of the
traditional Spanish names
are used throughout for
picking-hand fingers; using
numbers instead would
create confusion with the
fretting hand.

p (pulgar) = thumb
i (indice) = index
m (medio) = middle
a (anillo) = ring

Basic Strumming

1

○ track 02

Learning to play simple rhythms accurately and confidently is the key to building a rock-solid accompaniment.

It's important to play nice, wide strums for this exercise to ensure that the strings are played with equal weight. Here you can see the start of the down-strum with the pick about 10mm (⅜ inch) from the sixth string.

Strums should start and finish at roughly the same distance from the sixth and first strings respectively. Here, the down-strum has completed just 10mm (⅜ inch) past the first string before it returns to the starting position 10mm (⅜ inch) past the sixth string.

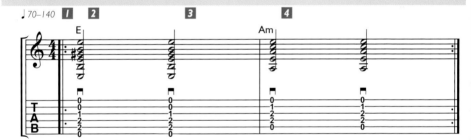

The E and Am chords are formed using exactly the same fingering shape but on different sets of strings. Aim to keep this shape intact when you release the pressure of your fretting hand.

Ideally the sixth string should be muted when playing the Am chord. You can achieve this by damping it with the tip of your thumb as shown here. If you find this awkward you can also try skipping over the sixth string with your pick to avoid sounding it (see Exercise 2).

track 03

Basic Strumming

2

Once you've mastered the half-note pattern, try adding an extra strum on beat 2 to create a more interesting rhythm.

After playing the third down-strum, play a ghosted down-strum (by lifting your pick clear of the strings) on the fourth beat as shown here. This will keep your strumming pattern grooving and consistent.

To avoid a nasty 'hole' in the rhythm, keep your fingers close to the strings when changing chords. This photograph along the strings illustrates how economical you can be with your finger movement.

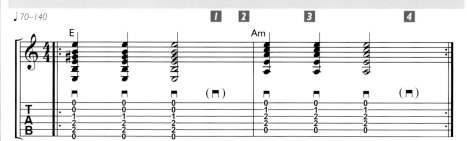

In addition to muting the sixth string when you play the Am, it's a good idea to also lift your pick clear of the string as shown here; this will achieve a tighter, more focused sound. However, don't change the starting point of your down-strum: this should still be 10mm (⅜ inch) from the sixth string.

In bar 2, the fourth beat should be played as a ghosted down-strum exactly as it was in the first bar. This will allow you to maintain a constant quarter-note strumming pattern (imagine your strumming arm is like the pendulum of a clock, moving evenly and consistently).

3 Basic Strumming

○ track 04

This exercise will teach you to change chords quickly and accurately without leaving any nasty 'gaps' in the rhythm.

To play consistent down-strums, make sure your silent up-strum (which returns the pick to its starting point) travels the same distance, at the same speed. Here the first up-stroke (beat 1) is shown at its finishing point 10mm (⅜ inch) from the sixth string.

Remember to keep that E/Am shape (it's the same shape for both chords) intact when you're changing chords. This will ensure that your change is smooth, efficient and, most importantly, without any unmusical 'gaps'.

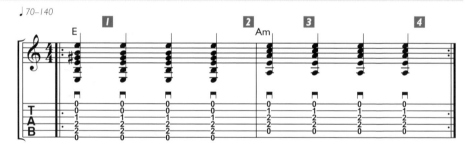

Keep your pick at 90 degrees to the strings on both down- and up-strums (it's important to make sure you don't start 'paintbrushing' in the direction that you're strumming). This will keep your rhythm work crisp and accurate.

In this exercise you will not only need to change quickly from E to Am, but also quickly back from Am to E on the repeat of the sequence. This photograph illustrates how the fingers remain as close as possible to the strings when changing chords.

The final basic strumming exercise will keep your fretting hand busy with two chord changes per bar, and includes half notes and quarter notes.

The first bar contains only half-note strums but it's a good idea to move your picking hand in a constant down/up pattern to achieve rhythmic consistency. The first bar should be played with a quarter-note strumming pattern (i.e. four down-strums per bar).

When changing from Em to Am, try to retain the shape of your second and third fingers. By moving them together you will only need to add your first finger to complete the Am shape as shown here.

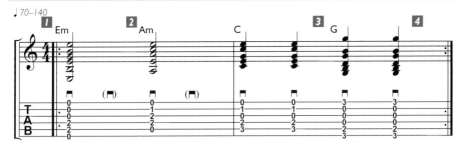

You will need to change chords quickly from C to G at the end of beat 2 in the second bar. You'll find this change is much easier when using the fingering shown here for the G chord. This fingering makes quick C to G (and vice versa) chord changes simple.

After playing the final G chord at the end of bar 2, keep your second finger in position on the second fret of the fifth string. Always remember to leave your fingers in position when changing chords if they don't need relocating.

5 Eighth-Note Strumming

track 06

Eighth-note strumming leaves little time for chord changes. This rhythm keeps things easy with quarter notes on the first and fourth beats.

Keep your pick moving down and up in a continuous eighth-note rhythm pattern throughout, playing ghosted up-strums on beats 1 and 4 in both bars, as indicated. This photograph illustrates the pick playing the first ghosted up-strum on beat 1 of bar 1.

In order to change quickly from Am to Em at the end of bar 1, keep your second and third fingers together as you move them. This will be tricky at first but, once you get the hang of it, you will be able to change chords more quickly and with much less effort.

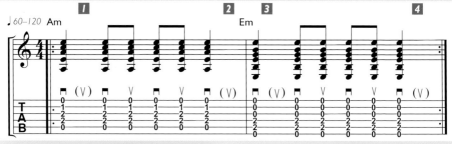

Remember to keep the distance that your pick travels consistent throughout. Here you can see the pick at the end of the down-strum on beat 1 of bar 2; notice how close the pick is to the high E (first) string. Keep your strumming tight and focused to achieve a rhythmic performance.

One of the trickiest parts of this exercise is getting your hands to move independently at the end of each bar. As the pick plays a ghosted up-strum at the end of bar 2, the fretting-hand fingers must simultaneously be performing the chord change back to Am as shown here.

This exercise teaches you how to avoid clumsy chord changes by simply strumming open strings at the end of each bar.

Make sure you're fretting your chord shape nice and cleanly before you start. Keeping your fingertips as close to 90 degrees as you can when fretting will help to prevent them from touching adjacent strings.

Keep your picking hand moving in a constant eighth-note rhythm throughout. It's important to keep the arc of your pick consistent on down- and up-strums. Here you can see the first up-strum at the end of its sweep, finishing quite close to the sixth string.

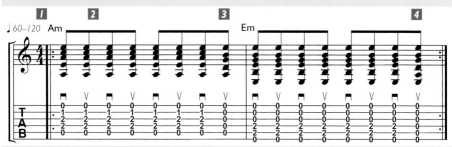

When you're playing a constant eighth-note rhythm, there's not much time for chord changes. So, do what the pros do and just hit the open strings! This photograph shows that the Am chord has been lifted off the strings while the picking hand would be playing an up-strum at the end of bar 1.

Similarly, at the end of bar 2, don't wait for the last up-strum before changing back to Am: there isn't enough time. As you're playing the final up-strum, simultaneously change chord shapes as shown here. You'll be surprised how effective this technique is once you've mastered it.

Eighth-Note Strumming

7

Learn how adding ties to a basic eighth-note strumming pattern will create syncopation that makes your rhythm work more interesting.

To prevent the chord from sounding muddy, the sixth string should be muted when playing the C chord. You can achieve this by damping it with the tip of your thumb as shown here.

This exercise adds a ghosted down-strum on the third beat. These are much harder to play than ghosted up-strums so take your time. Start slowly and make sure you keep counting throughout.

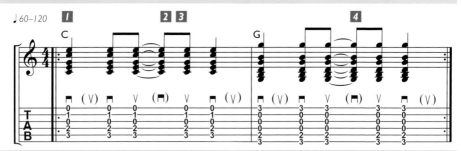

Keep your hand moving in a constant eighth-note rhythm when playing the ghosted down-strum on beat 3. This photograph illustrates the pick in position ready to play the up-strum that follows on the offbeat.

In bar 2, the third beat should be played as a ghosted down-strum exactly as it was in bar 1. By doing this you will avoid any disruption to the constant, pendulum-like strumming pattern, keeping your rhythm work clear and concise.

track 09

Eighth-Note Strumming

8

The slick, syncopated accompaniment rhythm in this exercise is a great rhythm pattern for playing on acoustic and electric alike.

This is how your pick should look at the start of the first up-strum. Keep your pick at 90 degrees to the strings, moving it upwards and gently sweeping across the strings without 'digging in'.

Immediately after each up-strum, the pick should begin its next down-strum. Ensure that your strums are not too 'wide': avoid moving any further than 10mm (⅜ inch) away from the sixth string. It's easier to maintain consistency with small, precise strums.

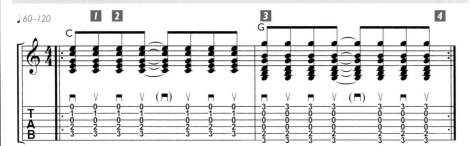

This constant eighth-note pattern adds up-strums on beats 1 and 4, meaning that there is very little time to change chords! Make sure you use the G chord fingering illustrated here (using the second and third fingers on the lowest strings) for a quick change.

Don't forget that you will also have to change quickly back to C on the repeat of the sequence. This photograph illustrates how the fingers remain as close as possible to the strings when changing chords, with the second and third fingers keeping the shape intact.

16th offbeat rhythms don't just sound great in reggae songs: they work really well in plenty of other styles, too.

The golden rule of rhythm playing is to keep your pick constantly moving down and up in the smallest subdivision used, in this case 16th notes. This photograph shows the pick playing a ghosted down-strum on beat 1 of the first bar.

Although only the top three strings are indicated in the TAB, form the full Am barre chord shape throughout the first barre. Releasing the grip of your fretting hand between strums (as shown here) will keep the strings muted.

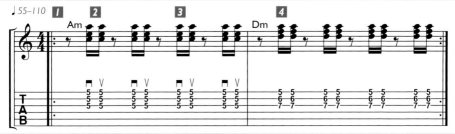

In order to sound only the top three strings of each chord, angle your strum so that it makes contact with the top strings only.

In the second bar, play the regular full Dm barre shape on the fifth fret as shown here. Just as in the first bar, you should release the grip of your fretting hands to play the rests between chords.

This power chord exercise is a heavy-metal groove often referred to as the 'Iron Maiden gallop' – and has been used by many bands.

The D5 power chord needs to be muted throughout; you can easily do this by lightly resting the palm of your picking hand on the fourth and fifth strings close to the bridge as shown here.

Remember that you're only playing two-note power chords so you don't need to strum across all six strings. This photograph shows the pick at the end of the first down-strum on beat 1. Notice that the pick stops just short of the third string.

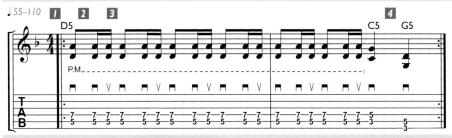

Similarly, your up-strum should finish at a similar distance from the fifth string. This photograph shows the last up-strum on beat 1, finishing just before it reaches the sixth string. Keep the arc of your strum narrow for best results.

When you change from C5 to G5, lift the first and third fingers off the strings but keep the chord shape intact as shown here. If you move the fingers individually or allow them to lose their shape, your chord change will be much slower and the chords will not ring for their full value.

11 16th-Note Strumming

The 'Bo Diddley Rhythm' is instant good-time rock 'n' roll. It's been used by everyone from George Michael to Prince – now it's your turn!

It's important to use the full six-string barre version of the G chord as shown here. Open chords don't work well with this rhythm as they make damping the chord (and playing percussive strums) impossible.

Maintain a constant 16th-note down/up strumming pattern throughout to achieve strong, musical results. Here the ghosted up-strum is being played just after the first G chord has been sounded on beat 1.

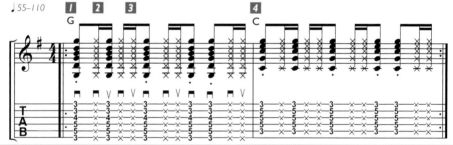

The cross-head notes represent muted notes that should be sounded. Instead of playing a ghosted stroke, strum the strings as you would normally. By releasing the pressure of your fretting hand without removing it from the strings (as shown here) you will create funky, percussive muted notes.

To facilitate a quick change to the C chord, use the fingering shown in this photograph. Notice that the first finger should fret only the fifth string: the barre is played with the third finger. Make sure you angle your third finger slightly at the first knuckle to prevent it from fretting the first string.

16th-Note Strumming **12**

This cool, syncopated funk rhythm has been featured in a lot of classic tracks, so it's definitely one you should learn.

Play the Am7 chord shape by forming a semi-barre across the higher strings with your third finger. By angling your second finger onto the fifth string (so that it gently rests on it), you will be able to keep it muted.

The secret to playing a grooving and consistent funk rhythm is to keep your strumming arm moving in a constant 16th-note down/up pattern. Here you can see the pick playing the ghosted down-strum on the offbeat of beat 1 when the 16th rest is played.

♩ 55–110 **1** Am7 **2** **3** **4** D9

To mute the strings, simply release the pressure of your fretting hand, allowing the fingers to relax their grip while remaining in contact with the strings. Funk players damp exclusively with their fretting hand, the opposite approach to a rock guitarist.

When changing to D9, release the pressure of your fretting hand and move the entire Am7 shape one set of strings higher (i.e. with the second finger moving to the fifth string). Then simply add your first finger on the fourth fret of the fourth string as shown here.

13 Basic Fingerpicking

This pinching exercise will help you to build a solid fingerstyle technique by getting you used to using your thumb and fingers simultaneously.

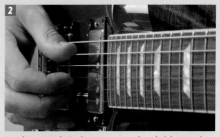

While striking the sixth string with your thumb (*p*), use your second finger (*m*) to simultaneously pick the second string. This technique is called 'pinching' because the thumb and fingers use a pinching motion to sound the strings.

For the second pinch, move your thumb (*p*) onto the fifth string, using your first finger (*i*) to pick the third string. The second finger (*m*) remains in position over the second string – keep fingers hovering over their respective strings even when they're not picking.

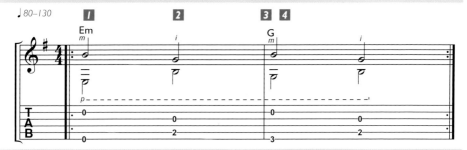

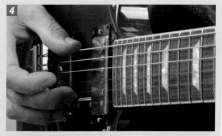

You don't always need to hold down a full chord shape when playing fingerstyle: here you can see only the lower notes of the G chord are fretted since the first string is not played.

At the start of bar 2, your thumb returns to the sixth string while your second finger (*m*) simultaneously picks the second string as before. Make sure you have the G chord shape fretted before you pick!

In this exercise you will learn how to play a bassline with your thumb while picking out a single note melody with your second finger.

Position your picking hand carefully before you start. You'll be playing the sixth string with your thumb (p) and the second string with your second finger (m) throughout, so it should be positioned as here.

The first two notes should be played as a pinching motion, the thumb striking the bass note downwards while the second finger picks the second string upwards. Keep your finger movements small to avoid losing your hand position.

♩ 60–120

Note: This exercise can also be played with bass notes on the fifth string and melody on the first string

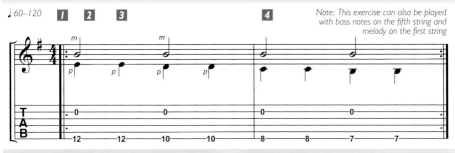

On the second beat only the bass note should be sounded. Although it may be tempting to rest your second finger on the second string as you play the bass note, avoid doing this as it will prevent the note from ringing for its full value.

Use your first finger to fret the C bass note in bar 2 as shown here. You can then slide the finger one fret lower for the final B bass note. On the repeat, jump back to E on the twelfth fret with your third finger.

Once you've got the hang of playing an independent bassline with your thumb, you can apply the technique to chords, too.

Before you play a note, make sure your picking hand is positioned as shown here. Note the claw-like shape of the hand and the angle of the wrist. The first (*i*), second (*m*) and third (*a*) fingers should be above the fourth, third and second strings respectively.

Pluck all four strings simultaneously and remember that the same 'pinching' motion (as used in Exercise 13) should also be used when using three picking-hand fingers and the thumb.

Keep the chord shape fretted on the second beat while playing the sixth-string bass note. This will allow the chord to sustain into the third beat, producing a smooth and consistent accompaniment.

When playing the bass note on the sixth string, move only your thumb and keep your picking hand steady with the fingers remaining in position above their respective strings.

Once you've mastered the previous exercise, try playing the chords on the offbeats to create a syncopated accompaniment.

As you play the first bass note with your thumb, your first (*i*), second (*m*) and third (*a*) fingers should be resting on their respective strings. Because the chords are punctuated by rests, you will be using your picking fingers to mute as well as to play the chords.

As you pick the first chord on the offbeat of beat 1, your thumb should simultaneously move onto the sixth string ready to play the next bass note. It's important to remember to keep your picking hand still when moving your thumb onto the sixth string.

♩60–100

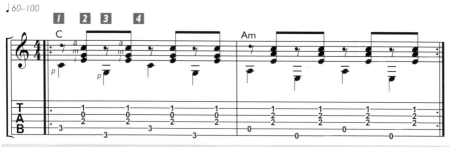

As soon as you've played the first chord, return your fingers to the strings as shown here. This keeps the chord short, as specified by the rest on the second beat (above the bass note).

You can make the bassline sound tighter and clearer by allowing the palm of your picking hand to gently rest on the fifth and sixth strings. This technique is known as palm muting and is used in fingerstyle guitar to prevent the bass notes from ringing simultaneously.

17 Eighth-Note Patterns

track 18

This indispensible 6/8 picking pattern can be applied to many different musical scenarios, from ballads to moderate tempo tunes.

'Let ring' means the chord shape should be held down for the full bar and each note should be allowed to ring on past its written length. Before you start, ensure that your picking hand is in position with each finger just above the relevant string.

There are no 'pinched' notes in this exercise: each note is sounded individually. Keep your picking hand still and move only the relevant finger. Avoid inadvertently muting any strings by keeping your thumb and fingers clear when not picking.

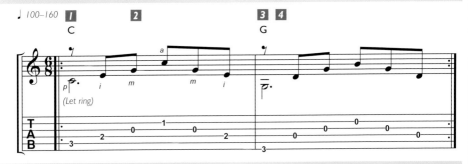

Always use the minimum number of fingers required to fret chords as this will make your changes quicker and smoother. Here, only the sixth string needs to be fretted when playing the G chord.

Keep your picking hand in a claw-like shape, using only your fingertips (or nails) to sound the strings. Your thumb should pick downwards while your fingers pick upwards with a 'pinching' motion.

This is a typical singer-songwriter style accompaniment from the folk scene of the 1960s, and a great picking-hand warm-up.

The exercise opens with a pinch on the first and fifth strings: strike the bass note with your thumb while simultaneously picking the first string with your third finger (a).

You'll notice that the C chord includes the high G note on the third fret: use your fourth finger to fret this note. Keep the finger in position until beat 3 to allow the note to continue ringing.

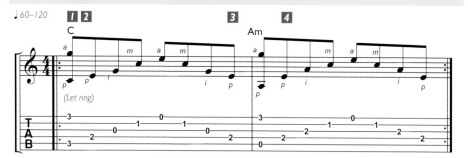

Your thumb plays all of the notes on the fourth string as well as the bass notes on the fifth string. Here, you can see the thumb playing the final note (E) in bar 1.

This pattern uses three picking-hand fingers, so keep your hand in the optimum position throughout. Here, the fingers (i, m and a) are poised over the top three strings while the thumb strikes the E in bar 2.

19 Eighth-Note Patterns

track 20

Create flowing, beautiful picking patterns by simply alternating between the thumb and fingers of your picking hand.

It's a good idea to start by practising the bassline first. You can then add the melody notes (stems up and picked with fingers) gradually. This photograph illustrates the thumb in position on the fourth string ready to play the second bass note (E).

Once you can play the bassline on autopilot you're ready to add the melody notes. These are syncopated, falling on the offbeats of the bass notes. Here, the first finger is picking the third string just after the thumb has played the bass note on the fifth string.

At the end of bar 1, allow the C note to ring on into the second bar by keeping your first and second fingers in position when changing to the Am chord. You only need to move your third finger when changing from C to Am (and vice versa).

To avoid having to look at your picking hand, remember to keep your hand in position above the strings as shown here. This way your fingers will always be poised and ready to pick, allowing you to play with greater confidence.

This simple-looking exercise mixes pinches, syncopation and a stride-style bassline to create an exciting picking pattern.

The D7 chord is the moveable version of the open C7 shape. Just fret a regular C7 chord and then move it two frets higher so that the lowest note falls on the fifth fret of the fifth string as shown here.

Here you can see the thumb picking the first bass note (D) while the second finger simultaneously picks the second string. Don't return your thumb: keep it hovering above the fourth string ready to play the next bass note.

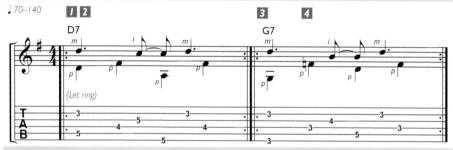

The G7 chord used in this exercise is the full barre shape but without the fourth finger on the second string. It's important to ensure that your third finger is maintained at a 90-degree angle to avoid inadvertently muting the fourth string.

To improve the clarity of the bassline (especially at higher tempos), lightly rest the palm of your picking hand on the bass strings to mute them. This prevents the notes from ringing into each other and keeps the bassline sounding tight and focused.

21 16th-Note Patterns

Although it looks complex, this syncopated 16th-note pattern is easy to play using just the thumb and first two fingers of your picking hand.

Fret the D5 chord using your first and third fingers as illustrated in this photograph. This may feel a little strange at first but it will make the chord change to D5/C much easier by leaving your second finger free to play the C bass note.

You'll only need your thumb, first and second picking-hand fingers to play this exercise. Here you can see the first finger is picking the third string while the second finger is poised above the second string ready to play the note that quickly follows.

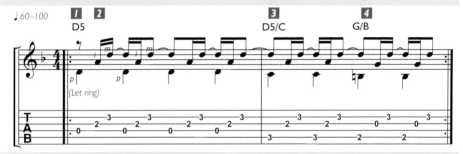

In the second bar, your thumb moves onto the fifth string to play the remaining bass notes. Make sure you move the thumb only, keeping your hand in the same position to allow the first and second fingers to stay above the third and second strings respectively.

To fret the G/B chord, simply move your first finger onto the fifth string while keeping your third finger in position. As you do so, ensure that you are not inadvertently muting the open third string, which must be allowed to ring clearly.

This is not just a cool-sounding picking pattern, it's also a great warm-up exercise for getting all your picking fingers up to speed.

Remember that when you're fingerpicking you don't have to fret the notes you won't be playing. So, because the fourth string of the C chord is not sounded, you don't have to fret it. Here, the chord is being fretted with just the first and third fingers.

This is a fast 16th-note pattern so your picking fingers need to be ready and in position above the relevant strings at all times. Here, the third string is being picked with the first finger, and the second and third fingers are already in position above the strings.

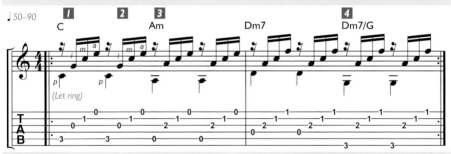

Since the fourth string is not sounded, you can fret the Am chord with just your first and second fingers, as shown here. This also facilitates a quick change to the Dm7 in the second bar.

As your thumb moves onto the sixth string to play the bass note of the Dm7/G chord, make sure you keep your three picking-hand fingers in position above their respective strings. This will avoid any picking errors and will enable you to play without having to constantly look at your picking hand.

23 16th-Note Patterns

track 24

Applying 16th-note picking patterns to a 6/8 pulse can create beautifully hypnotic accompaniments, as demonstrated in this exercise.

Throughout this exercise, your picking-hand fingers should remain in the same position. Here is the correct positioning, with the thumb about to strike the fifth string while the first, second and third fingers are poised above the fourth, third and second strings.

Although the G/B chord notes could be picked out of a full G chord shape (with a D added on the second string), it's more efficient to fret the notes that will be played, in this case the low B and the high D, as shown here, with only the second and fourth fingers.

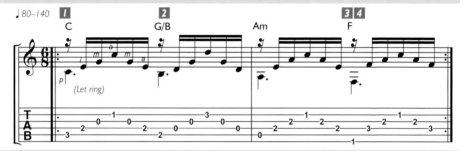

Always fret your bass notes first: this avoids creating unmusical 'gaps', especially at brighter tempos. Notice how the low F chord can be quickly formed but without pressing all the notes onto the frets; it is only necessary to fret the bass note immediately.

Without disrupting the position of your picking-hand fingers, move your thumb onto the sixth string ready to play the first note of the F chord in bar 2. Remember to keep your picking fingers in position above their respective strings throughout.

16th-Note Patterns

24

This exercise uses an eighth-note, alternating-bass pattern against syncopated melody notes to create an exciting 'double time' groove.

It's important to keep your picking hand totally still when playing alternating-bass patterns. Here you can see the ideal hand position: the thumb is picking the sixth string while the first and second fingers are in position above the third and second strings.

By lightly resting your palm on the bass strings close to the bridge, you will be able to keep your hand in position while also lightly muting the bass notes to improve the clarity and definition of the bassline.

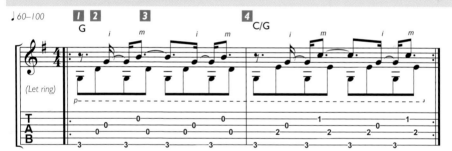

The melody notes should never be picked simultaneously with a bass note, as this would spoil the pattern's syncopated rhythm. Here you can see that as the second finger (*m*) picks the second string, the thumb moves across to strike the open D string.

To fret the C/G chord, add your first and second fingers while allowing your third and fourth fingers to remain in position from the G chord. Hold down the chord shape to allow all the notes to ring into each other. This photo illustrates the correct fingering.

25 Eighth-Note Picking

Because you'll be using all four fretting-hand fingers, this exercise makes a great warm-up routine for getting all your fingers working efficiently.

Before you start, position your hand on the fingerboard with all fingers pressing on the frets as shown. As you lift off your fingers, keep them as close to the strings as possible; the most efficient technique looks effortless because there is no wasted movement.

Keep your picking arc quite narrow to avoid unnecessary and excessive picking-hand movement. This photograph illustrates the pick at the end of the first down-pick, just after playing the first note (A).

♩ 70–120

Note: You can play this exercise on any string

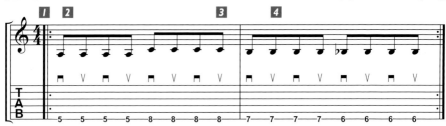

Don't waste energy removing the fingers from the frets; keep them in position (this will save you re-fretting each note in the second bar). Here the fourth finger frets the C at the end of the first bar with all of the other fingers still in position on their respective frets.

Notice that the up-picks should all fall on the offbeats. In this photograph the pick is playing an up-pick on the offbeat of beat 1, bar 2. It's important to maintain this pattern of 'down-picks on the beat, up-picks off the beat' in order to develop an accurate and rhythmic alternate-picking technique.

Eighth-Note Picking

26

In this exercise you will learn to apply alternate picking, while moving between the fifth and sixth strings.

The first note should be played with a down-pick. Try to avoid looking at your pick when you change strings: it's much better to practise slowly and build your confidence gradually than to learn bad habits.

After playing the fourth A note in bar 1 with an up-pick, your pick will need to travel back across the sixth string ready to play the D on the fifth string on beat 3.

♩ 70–120   Note: You can also play this exercise starting on the fifth, fourth, third and second strings

Similarly, at the end of bar 1 your pick will need to skip back over the sixth string ready to play the B in bar 2 with a down-pick. This movement may seem confusing at first but it will soon become automatic and you will no longer have to think about your picking when moving across strings.

Instead of lifting your third finger off the sixth string and placing it back onto the fifth string to play the E on beat 3 of bar 2, flatten your finger across the fifth string as shown here. This technique is known as 'finger rolling' and it's great for fretting adjacent strings quickly.

27 Eighth-Note Picking

track 28

The minor pentatonic scale is familiar to most guitar players, so it's the obvious first scale choice when applying alternate picking technique.

Although many blues players use their first and third fingers only to play this scale, it's good practice to use your fourth finger to fret all of the notes on the eighth fret. This will help you to build fourth-finger strength and independence.

When ascending through the scale in bar 1, the first note on each string should start with a down-pick. Here, you see the pick correctly playing the fourth string on beat 3 (G) with a down-pick.

♩ 70–120 **A minor pentatonic shape 1** *Note: You can transpose this exercise to other keys by starting on a different fret*

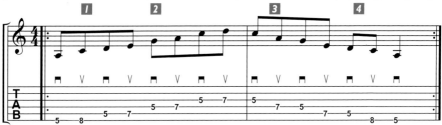

In bar 2 the picking pattern is slightly more complex and the down- and up-picks don't fall on the same string. This means that after each down-pick the pick has to travel back across the string it has just played before it can play an up-pick. Here, the pick skips over the third string to play the first up-pick in bar 2.

Aim to maximise economy of movement by moving your fretting-hand fingers as little as possible. The further away from the strings they move, the longer it takes to fret notes. Here, the first finger frets the D on the fifth string with the fourth finger in position, ready to play the C on the eighth fret.

Eighth-Note Picking

28

Major scale patterns contain both two and three notes per string, making them a little more challenging to play with alternate picking.

As always, make sure your fretting hand is in a good position before you start: the first note of the scale should be fretted with your second finger as shown here. Notice how the remaining fingers are also in position above their respective frets.

Remember that when you're using alternate picking, onbeat notes will always be played with a down-pick and offbeat notes will always be played with an up-pick. Here you can see the second note (D) being correctly played with an up-pick.

♩ 70–120   **C major scale shape I**   *Note: You can transpose this exercise to other keys by starting on a different fret*

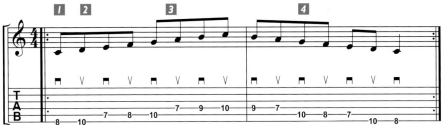

On beat 3 of bar 1, the down- and up-picks no longer fall on the same string. This means that after playing the first note (G), the down-pick will need to continue across the fourth string in order to be in position to play the following A note with an up-pick.

As you progress through the scale, don't neglect your fretting hand! The G at the start of beat 2, bar 2 is played with your fourth finger, and the first and second fingers are in position above their respective frets ready to play the following F and E notes.

Triplet alternate picking reverses your picking pattern on every other beat, so can be confusing. This exercise will help you get to grips with it.

Remember that your optimum fretting-hand position requires all your fingers to be in position as shown. As you lift off your fingers, keep them as close to the strings as possible; the further you move off the strings, the further you'll need to move back to re-fret.

Your picking arc should be narrow for maximum economy of movement. This photograph illustrates the pick at the end of the first down-pick, just after playing the first note on beat 1 (G).

♩ 60–110

Note: You can play this exercise on any string

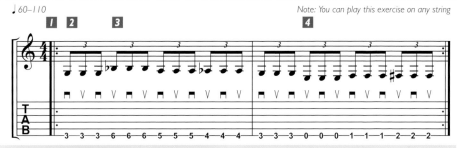

On the second beat, your picking pattern will reverse from down/up/down to up/down/up. This is necessary to avoid playing consecutive down-picks. Once you've got the hang of this, try accenting the first note on every beat.

As you play the open E on beat 2 of the second bar, move your fretting hand into position as shown, with the first and second fingers above the first and second frets. On the repeat, play the first note of bar 1 (G) with your first finger to return your hand to third position.

You will have heard this classic triplet pentatonic pattern in many blues and rock solos. It's great for building your triplet-picking technique.

Although many blues and rock players only use their first and third fingers to play minor pentatonic scales, start with your fourth finger on the eighth fret as shown here for maximum technique building.

As you pick down to play the final C note on beat 1, allow your pick to travel past the fifth string after striking the sixth string as shown here. This will move it into position ready to play the D on beat 2 with an up-pick.

♩ 60–110   A minor pentatonic shape 1   Note: You can transpose this exercise to other keys by starting on a different fret

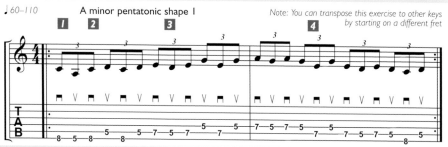

To build the most efficient fretting-hand technique, always avoid moving your fingers too far from the strings, even when they are not in use. Here you can see the first and third fingers in action playing the notes on beat 3, with the unused second and fourth fingers remaining close to the strings.

On beat 2 of bar 2, allow the first up-pick to travel past the fifth string after playing the G on the fourth string as shown in this photograph. This will move your pick into position ready to play the following E note with a down-pick.

31 Triplets

○ track 32

This is an exercise spanning two octaves of the A minor pentatonic scale. It will really get your triplet picking up to speed.

Remember the golden rule: get your fretting hand in position before you start! The first note (A) should be fretted with your first finger as shown here. Notice that the fourth finger is already in position above the eighth fret ready to play the second note.

Every time you move to a higher string, the first note should be played with a down-pick. Try to avoid naturally accenting these notes; instead accent the first note of each beat. Here, the fifth string is being picked with an (accented) up-pick on beat 2.

♩ 60–110   A minor pentatonic shape I

Note: You can transpose this exercise to other keys by starting on a different fret

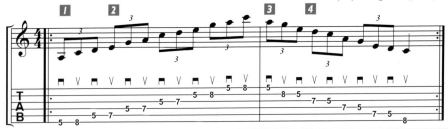

In order to play these patterns efficiently (and increase your speed), your fingers need to 'think ahead' to the next note. In this photograph, the first note of bar 2 is fretted with the first finger while the fourth finger simultaneously moves into position ready for the next note on the second string.

On the second beat of bar 2, the preceding down-pick first needs to travel back across the second string before playing the D note with an up-pick as shown here. These wider pick arcs may seem awkward at first but they will soon become second nature with regular practice.

This shape-one C major scale pattern is an ideal vehicle for testing your newly acquired triplet-picking technique.

The first note of this scale should be fretted with your second finger as shown here. Notice how the remaining fingers are also in position above their respective frets: this is the only way to build speed and accuracy.

On beat 2 your picking pattern will reverse from down/up/down to up/down/up. Avoid accenting down-picks that fall on a new string (as at the end of beat 1). Instead, accent the first note of each beat. Here you see the accented up-pick on beat 2.

♩ 60–110   C major scale shape I

Note: You can transpose this exercise to other keys by starting on a different fret

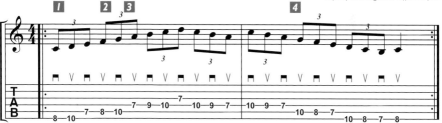

On beat 2 of bar 1, the down- and up-picks no longer fall on the same string when playing the G and A notes. After playing the G your down-pick will need to continue past the fourth string in order to be in position to up-pick the following A note.

The situation is reversed when descending the scale in the second bar. Here you can see that, after playing the A at the end of beat 1, the down-pick has to skip back across the fourth string ready to play the G on beat 2 with an up-pick.

33 16th-Note Picking

By avoiding any string changes, this 16th-note exercise is perfect for warming up your picking hand.

Before you begin, position your fretting hand as demonstrated in this photograph. The first finger is fretting the first note (A) while the remaining fingers are positioned directly above their respective frets.

When using 16th-note alternate picking, your pick should travel the shortest distance possible to keep muscle movement to a minimum. This photograph illustrates the pick at the end of the first down-pick, just after playing the first note on beat 1 (A).

♩ 60–100

Note: You can play this exercise on any string

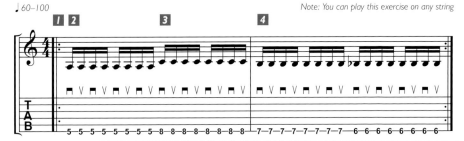

Each new four-note grouping should start with a down-pick. This photograph illustrates the first note on the third beat (C) being correctly played with a down-pick. Notice that when you're using 16th-note picking, the second and fourth notes only (the offbeats) should be picked with an up-pick.

Notice that when you are fretting the first note (B) in bar 2, it's a good idea to also fret the sixth fret with your second finger as shown here, ready for the B♭ in beat 3. This will avoid any unmusical hesitation between note changes.

Chromatic-scale patterns are perfect for warming up your 16th-note alternate-picking technique, so make this part of your daily routine!

Since you'll be using all four of your fretting-hand fingers in this exercise, optimise your hand position before you start. Here, the first finger is fretting the first note (A) while the other fingers span the next three frets, ready for the notes that quickly follow.

As you ascend through this scale, you'll notice that the last note on each string is an up-pick. This photograph shows the pick skipping back over the string it has just played ready to play the down-pick on the third string on beat 2.

♩=60–100   Chromatic scale starting on A   *Note: Try the same pattern starting on a different fret*

The accents in the first bar fall naturally at the start of each beat. Here the A on beat 4 is played with an accented down-pick.

The pattern of four notes per string is disrupted when descending the scale so you'll need to place your accents more carefully – they will no longer coincide with a string change. Here you can see the accented down-pick playing the first note (G) on beat 2, even though this is the second note on the second string.

35　16th-Note Picking

track 36

The two-octave A minor pentatonic scale can be played quickly and accurately using an alternate 16th-note picking technique.

This familiar pattern is often wrongly played using only the first and third fingers of your fretting hand. Although it's easy to play this way, you'll overlook your fourth finger (here fretting the second note on the eighth fret) and establish bad habits.

Every time you move to a higher string, play the first note with a down-pick. Try to avoid accenting these notes; instead only accent the first note of each beat. Here you can see the fourth string correctly sounded with an accented down-pick on beat 2.

♩ 60–100　　　　　　　A minor pentatonic shape 1　　Note: You can transpose this exercise to other keys by starting on a different fret

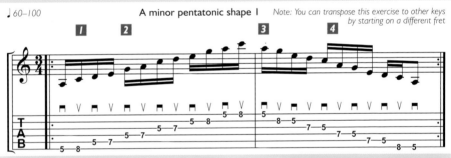

Remember that your fingers must always be one step ahead when you're playing 16th-note scale patterns. In this photograph, the first note of bar 2 is fretted with the first finger while the fourth finger moves into position ready for the next note on the second string.

On the second beat of bar 2, the down-pick needs to skip back across the third string before playing the A note with an up-pick as shown here. It's best to play all of this exercise without looking at your picking hand, even if it means mistakes are initially made.

16th-Note Picking

36

Mixing two- and three-notes-per-string patterns, the major scale is the perfect challenge to take your alternate picking to the max!

The first note of this scale should be fretted with your second finger as shown here. Notice how the remaining fingers are also in position above their respective frets. Remember that this is the only way to build speed and accuracy.

Notice that you'll move onto the fifth string on the third note (E). It's important to avoid accenting this note, although it will feel natural to do so. Instead accent the first note on beat 2, which should be played with a down-pick as shown here.

♩ 60–100   **C major scale shape 1**

Note: You can transpose this exercise to other keys by starting on a different fret

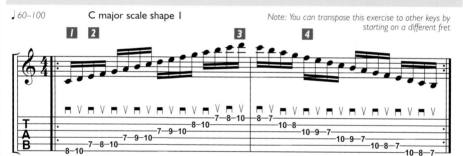

This photograph illustrates the last note (D) in bar 1 fretted with the fourth finger. Notice how the first and second fingers are also still fretting the previous notes (B and C). This will save having to re-fret the notes when descending the scale in bar 2.

It's only on the second beat that you'll find a string change that coincides with an accented down-pick, as illustrated here. For this reason you'll need to take extra care when applying accents: they must only be applied at the start of each beat.

Using chromatic-approach notes to the minor pentatonic scale, this exercise will get your first and second fretting fingers up to speed.

To hammer-on to a higher note, pick the first note only. The second note's sound is generated only by the impact of your finger hitting the fingerboard – hence the technique's name.

As you pick the first note, your second finger should already be in position above the sixth fret for the hammer-on to the second note. Notice that the first finger frets snugly behind the fifth fret.

♩ 60–150

G minor pentatonic shape 1

Note: You can transpose this exercise to other keys by starting on a different fret

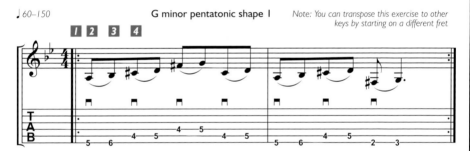

As you play the hammer-on, make sure your second finger makes contact with the string quickly and accurately. It should fret the string as close as possible to the sixth fret as shown here.

Although it's a good idea to also play this exercise using up-picks too, you will achieve the clearest slurs by picking the strings with down-picks throughout as shown here.

Give your third and fourth fretting-hand fingers a thorough workout with this minor-pentatonic-based exercise.

Ensure that your fretting hand is correctly positioned, as shown here, before you start. Notice that the first finger should be positioned closely behind the third fret while the fourth finger is suspended above the sixth fret.

Your fourth finger must make contact just behind the sixth fret to ensure the higher note is audible. Your first finger must remain in position (and pressed hard onto the fingerboard) or the string will be muted and the 'hammered' note will not sound.

♩ 60–150   **G minor pentatonic shape I**   *Note: You can transpose this exercise to other keys by starting on a different fret*

As soon as you've successfully sounded the hammer-on, your first finger should be moving across to the next string before you release the fourth finger.

Ensure that your third finger 'hammers' onto the guitar neck just behind the fifth fret. Your ultimate goal is to make the slurred notes sound just as loud as the picked notes.

Applying a legato technique to the major scale involves playing double hammer-ons, where only the first of three notes is picked.

The first note of this scale should be fretted with your second finger as shown here. Notice how the fourth finger is also in position above the tenth fret; always ensure that your 'hammer-on' finger is in position before playing the first note.

On the second beat, the first note of a three-note hammer-on is played on the fifth string. It's important to ensure that your three fretting-hand fingers are correctly positioned as shown here.

♩ 60–150

C major scale shape 1

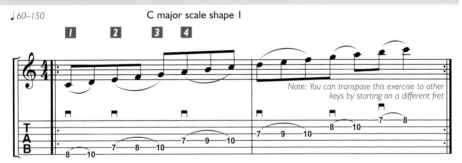

Note: You can transpose this exercise to other keys by starting on a different fret

Keep your fingers on the strings as you hammer-on each new note – this will ensure the string continues to ring clearly. Here you can see the first and second fingers fretting the fifth string while the fourth finger prepares to hammer-on the third note (G).

Just as in the previous hammer-on exercises, use strong down-picks to sound the strings throughout, especially when executing three-notes-per-string hammer-ons.

Hammer-on Exercises

40

For the ultimate hammer-on workout, the chromatic scale enables four-notes-per-string slurs to be played.

Make sure you use your first finger to fret the first note (C) as shown here. Notice how the remaining fingers are also in position above their respective frets: this is the only way to successfully execute multiple hammer-ons.

Keep your fingers pressed firmly down on the strings as you hammer-on each note so the string continues to ring clearly. Here, the first, second and third fingers fret the sixth string while the fourth finger prepares to hammer-on the fourth note (D♯).

♩ 60–110   Chromatic scale starting on C

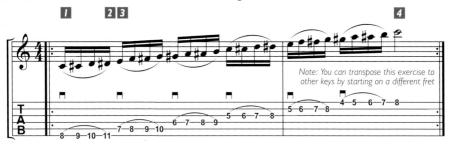

Note: You can transpose this exercise to other keys by starting on a different fret

As soon as your fourth finger has successfully fretted the fourth note, lift your first finger off the sixth string and move it back a fret and onto the fifth string ready for the start of the next series of hammer-ons.

To play the final C at the end of the second bar, release the pressure of your fretting-hand fingers and slide your hand one fret position higher. Your fourth finger will now be in position on the eighth fret as shown here.

Pull-off Exercises

41

This exercise focuses entirely on your first and second fretting-hand fingers, allowing you to improve your slurring technique gradually.

When applying pull-off technique to fretted notes, both notes must be fretted simultaneously before you pick the string. This photograph shows the first pull-off in bar 1 with both the first and second fingers in position ready to start the exercise.

Here you can see the second finger after being lifted off the string to sound the second note (A). Notice that it has come to rest above the fifth string because you need to release your finger with a sideways 'flicking' motion to generate the lower note.

♩ 60–150   **G minor pentatonic shape I**   *Note: You can transpose this exercise to other keys by starting on a different fret*

Remember that you will only be picking the first of each pair of notes; you will be 'pulling' your finger off the string to generate the second. Here you can see the fifth string being played with a down-pick on beat 2.

To play the final pair of notes, your hand will need to move down to third position, allowing your second finger to fret the fourth fret as shown here. Notice how the first finger is also fretting the third fret ready for the pull-off.

track 43

Pull-off Exercises

42

Develop a confident pull-off technique with your third and fourth fretting-hand fingers using this minor-pentatonic-based exercise.

Always ensure that both fretting-hand fingers are in position and pressing down firmly on the fingerboard (snugly behind their respective frets) before you pick the string, as shown here.

Flick your fourth finger sideways as you release it from the string to create the first pull-off. Lifting your finger straight off the string will fail to generate the second pitch.

♩ 60–150

G minor pentatonic shape I

Note: You can transpose this exercise to other keys by starting on a different fret

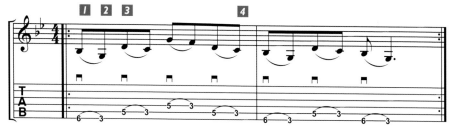

As soon as you've successfully sounded the pull-off, you should be moving your fingers into position on the next string. This photograph shows the third finger moving across to the fifth string while the low G note is still ringing on the first beat.

At the end of bar 1, stretch your fourth finger so that it can move into position ready for the next note (B♭) on the sixth string. It's important to keep your hand still as you do so to avoid losing your position on the neck.

43 Pull-off Exercises

track 44

This descending exercise involves some challenging three-notes-per-string pull-offs that will help you to develop a powerful legato technique.

The first note of this scale should be fretted with your second finger as shown here. Notice how the first finger is also in position on the seventh fret; always ensure that your 'pull-off' finger is in position before picking the first note.

On the third beat, the first note of a three-note pull-off is played on the third string. It's important to ensure that all three fretting-hand fingers are fretting their respective frets before you pick the string, as shown here.

♩ 60–150

C major scale shape I

Note: You can transpose this exercise to other keys by starting on a different fret

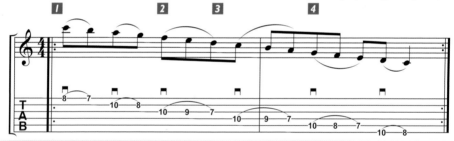

Remember that each finger must be released with a sideways 'flicking' motion in order to sound the new note. Here you can see the third finger after releasing to sound the D on beat 4.

As in the previous exercises, use down-picks throughout to play only the first note of each note grouping. This is the best way to produce a strong, clear note. Once you can do this you can experiment with up-picks too.

    Pull-off Exercises   **44**

For the ultimate pull-off workout, the chromatic scale enables four-notes-per-string slurs to be played.

Keep your thumb in position on the back of the neck as shown here. This will offer the best support for your fingers and allow you to execute precise pull-offs.

Make sure you use your fourth finger to fret the first note (C) as shown here. Notice how the remaining fingers are already pressing down on their respective frets – this is the only way to successfully execute multiple pull-offs.

♩ 60–110   **Chromatic scale starting on C**   *Note: You can transpose this exercise to other keys by starting on a different fret*

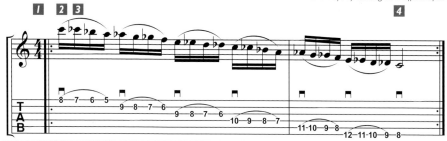

Keep your remaining fingers in position, pressing firmly down on the strings as you release each finger, to ensure the string continues to ring clearly. Here you can see the first, second and third fingers in position while the fourth finger plays the first pull-off.

To play the final C, release the pressure of your fretting-hand fingers and slide your hand one fret position lower. Your first finger should now be in position on the eighth fret, as shown here.

45 Combining Slurs

By combining hammer-ons and pull-offs, you will be able to create flowing lines with ease, as this exercise illustrates.

Don't forget that the second note of the minor pentatonic should be played with your fourth finger. Here you can see the first note (A) being fretted with the first finger while the fourth finger hovers in position above the eighth fret.

On beat 3 of bar 1, play a consecutive hammer-on/pull-off with your first and third fingers. Hammer your third finger into position close behind the seventh fret (as shown), then release the finger by flicking sideways to regenerate the lower note.

♩ 70–150

A minor pentatonic shape 1

Note: You can transpose this exercise to other keys by starting on a different fret

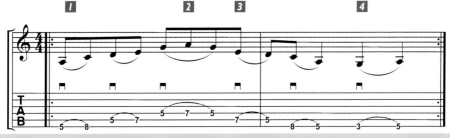

Although the final note in the first bar falls on the offbeat, you will achieve a stronger pull-off by picking with a down-pick and ignoring the eighth-note alternate-picking rule (see Exercise 25).

For the penultimate note (G), move your hand down the neck into third position so that you can play this with your first finger. Notice how the third finger is in position above the fifth fret ready to play the hammer-on.

Fast 16th-note scale patterns are easy to play when you use hammer-ons to ascend and pull-offs to descend.

In this exercise you should use down-picks throughout to play each pair of slurs. In this example, none of the picked notes fall on offbeat 16th notes so you will effectively be applying 16th-note alternate picking.

Remember that as you hammer-on the second note on each string, your finger should make contact with the string firmly and accurately, ideally directly behind the relevant fret. Here you can see the third finger hammering onto the seventh fret on beat 2.

♩60–120

A minor pentatonic shape 1   *Note: You can transpose this exercise to other keys by starting on a different fret*

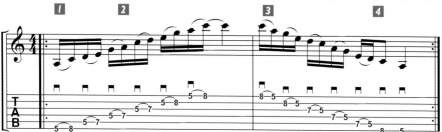

To execute a pull-off successfully, remember that your first finger must also be in position on the fifth fret, as shown here. It's very important to use the sideways flicking motion when releasing your finger, otherwise the lower pitch will sound thin and quiet.

Encourage your fingers to 'think ahead' at all times. Here you can see the fourth finger moving into position on the eighth fret, while the lower note of the pull-off (D) is still sounding on beat 3 of bar 2.

Introducing syncopated hammer-ons and pull-offs into a pentatonic phrase can create exciting, fast licks that will enhance any solo.

On the third beat of bar 1, use your first and fourth fingers to execute the consecutive hammer-on/pull-off (remembering not to pick the higher note). The fourth finger should be released with a sideways flicking motion as illustrated.

Because the G that immediately follows falls on a syncopated note, play this note with an up-pick, as shown here.

♩ 60–120   A minor pentatonic shape 1

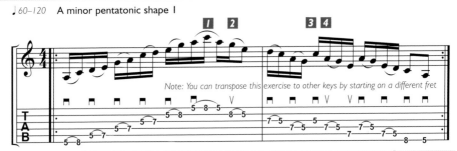

Note: You can transpose this exercise to other keys by starting on a different fret

In bar 2, to move quickly from the G at the end of beat 1 to the C on beat 2, don't lift your first finger off the fret. Instead, flatten it across the strings to form a semi-barre as this photograph illustrates.

Notice that the next two notes on this beat are played with up-picks: this will not only help you to keep your phrasing rhythmically accurate, it will also make it much easier to play the quick down-pick on beat 3, particularly at higher tempos.

Combining Slurs

48

It is easier to play major scales (and modes) legato when using three-notes-per-string. This exercise shows you how.

It's vital to ensure your hand is positioned with your fingers above their respective frets before you start. The first finger is in position fretting the first note, with the second and fourth fingers above the tenth and twelfth frets respectively.

Despite some of the picked notes falling on offbeats, it is best to use down-picks throughout. You will, however, need to ensure that you don't allow the three-notes-per-string to turn into triplets; 16th-note groupings must be adhered to by using a metronome.

♩ 70–120   C major scale shape 1 and shape 2 combined

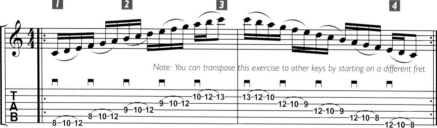

Note: You can transpose this exercise to other keys by starting on a different fret

The eighth note at the end of bar 1 enables you to pause momentarily before re-picking the note and starting your descent. Remember that you must have all three fingers in position before you pick the string, as shown here.

Remember that a pull-off won't generate the lower pitch successfully unless you release each finger with a sideways flicking motion. This photograph shows the fourth finger at rest above the fifth string, having just played the first pull-off on beat 4 of bar 2.

49   Note Groupings

track 50

Note groupings will help you to learn scales in a realistic and challenging format. They're great fun to play too!

Use the alternate eighth-note picking indicated throughout this exercise. This photograph shows the second note on the sixth string (C) being correctly played with an up-pick.

After ascending the first four notes of the scale (hence this pattern's name), you will return to the second note and ascend the next four notes. Here you can see the fourth finger hovering over the eighth fret ready to play the C on beat 3.

♩ 70–150   A minor pentatonic shape 1 – 'four-in-a-line' (ascending)

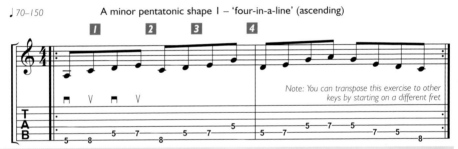

Note: You can transpose this exercise to other keys by starting on a different fret

Keep your fretting hand steady, with the fingers positioned above their respective frets throughout this exercise. This will minimise the time it takes you to fret each new note.

After playing the final note (G) in bar 1, your up-pick will need to travel twice its normal distance in order to skip back over the fifth string. Here you can see the pick back in position on beat 1, bar 2, ready to play the first note (D).

Note Groupings

50

To get maximum benefit from any note grouping, you must practise the pattern ascending and descending. This exercise shows you how.

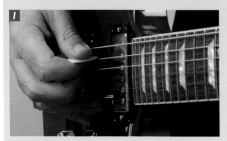

It's important to adhere to the alternate 16th-note picking indicated throughout this exercise so you can improve your technique in both hands. This photograph shows the third note of bar 1 (D) being correctly played with a down-pick.

Here you can see the C on beat 2 being fretted with the fourth finger. Notice how close the finger is to the fret: this produces a nice clear note with no nasty fret buzz.

♩ 60–120   A minor pentatonic shape I – 'four-in-a-line' (ascending and descending)

Note: You can transpose this exercise to other keys by starting on a different fret

After playing the A at the end of beat 3, bar 1, your up-pick will need to skip back over the fourth string before it can play the E that follows. Here you can see the pick back in position and ready to play the note on beat 4 with a down-pick.

Encourage your fingers to 'think ahead' at all times. Here you can see the fourth finger hovering above the eighth fret ready to play the last note in bar 2, while the first finger frets the D on the fifth string.

51 Note Groupings

track 52

The major scale (and its related modes) is ideal for practising note groupings. Some of these patterns are great for creating licks, too.

You'll use all of your fretting-hand fingers for this exercise, so make sure your fingers are in position before you start. Here, the second finger frets the first note (C) while the first finger hovers above the seventh fret, fifth string, ready for the second note.

Use the alternate 16th-note picking indicated on the first beat, throughout this exercise. Here you can see the third note of bar 1 (D) being correctly played with a down-pick.

♩ 60–120   C major scale shape 1 – '1-3-2-1' (ascending)

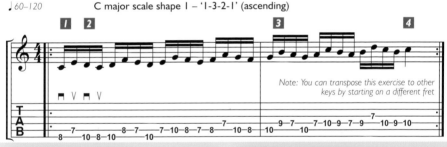

Note: You can transpose this exercise to other keys by starting on a different fret

In bar 2, the first two notes (G and B) should be played with your fourth and third fingers respectively. These two fingers are often the hardest to move independently so take your time; don't fall into the trap of notching up the tempo too quickly.

The final note (C) should be played with your fourth finger as illustrated. Remember that this note is a whole beat (quarter note) long, so you'll have plenty of time to return to the first note on the sixth string when repeating.

Note Groupings

52

In this exercise, you'll learn how to apply the previous note grouping as a descending pattern. Why not try combining both exercises?

Because the first three notes are all located on the fourth string, you can fret all of them before you start. Here you can see the first, third and fourth fretting-hand fingers already in position on their respective frets.

As with all of the exercises in this section, use the alternate 16th-note picking indicated on the first beat, throughout. Here you can see the second note of bar 1 (A) being correctly sounded with an up-pick.

♩ *60–120*   C major scale shape 1 – '1-3-2-1' (descending)

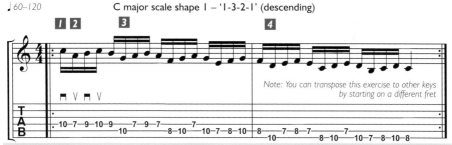

Note: You can transpose this exercise to other keys by starting on a different fret

The second note (G) on beat 2 moves straight to the fifth string, tenth fret. This tricky move involves good independence between the fingers so it may take a little practice to execute smoothly.

In bar 2, after picking the first note with a down-pick, your pick will need to travel back across the fifth string before being able to play the following note (D) with an up-pick.

53 Intervals

This basic minor-pentatonic exercise in fourths will help you to develop a solid picking and fretting technique. Try other scales in fourths, too.

The most efficient way to fret notes on adjacent strings is to use 'finger rolling'. Instead of lifting your finger on and off, simply roll it onto the higher string. Keep your finger in contact with both strings, releasing the pressure on the lower string to mute it.

Use eighth-note picking throughout, as indicated in bar 1. Here you can see the pick correctly playing the second note (D) with an up-pick.

♩ 70–150

A minor pentatonic shape 1 – fourths

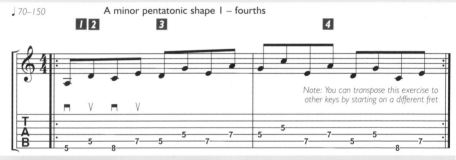

Note: You can transpose this exercise to other keys by starting on a different fret

Even though you won't be using your second finger, it's good practice to keep all your fingers close to the frets throughout this exercise. This will ensure that you develop a rock-solid fretting-hand technique.

Continue to apply the finger-rolling technique as you descend back down the scale. This photograph illustrates the third finger rolling onto the fourth string after playing the E on beat 2 of bar 2.

Intervals

54

Double-stacked fourths are great fun to play both with regular- and economy-picking techniques.

Economy picking can be used to play all three notes in each triplet; this takes practice and patience but it's a technique worth persevering with. This shot shows the down-pick on beat 1 that will 'sweep' across the sixth, fifth and fourth strings in one move.

The first three notes all fall on the same fret so use finger rolling to play them. Here, the first finger is falling across the strings to sound the notes. Don't barre across the strings: your finger should roll as you pick, applying fretting pressure to one string at a time.

A minor pentatonic shape I – stacked fourths

Note: You can transpose this exercise to other keys by starting on a different fret

If you're using conventional alternate picking to play these notes, remember that on the second and fourth beats, the first note of each triplet will start with an up-pick. In this photograph the pick is correctly playing the first note on beat 2 with an up-pick.

On the second beat of bar 2, only the first two notes will be played using finger rolling (in this case with the third finger); the last note (G) on the second string should be fretted with your fourth finger. Keep the third finger resting on the lower strings as shown here.

55 Intervals

This major scale in thirds not only sounds great, it's also a great exercise for building your chops.

You'll use all of your fretting-hand fingers for this exercise so position your fingers before you start. Here you can see the second finger fretting the first note (C) while the first finger hovers above the fifth string, seventh fret, ready for the second note.

Throughout this exercise, use the alternate 16th-note picking indicated on the first beat. Here you can see the fourth note of bar 1 (F) being correctly played with an up-pick.

♩ 60–120   C major scale shape 1 – thirds

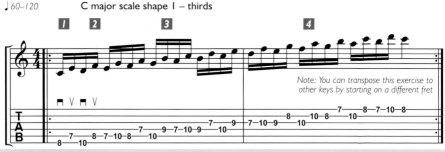

Note: You can transpose this exercise to other keys by starting on a different fret

Try to always keep your fingers as close to the strings as possible, even when they are not being used. Here the third finger frets the second note on beat 3 (B) while the unused fingers keep close to the strings, ready to play the notes that follow.

On the second beat of bar 2, use the finger-rolling technique with your fourth finger to play both the F and A notes. This is the hardest finger to control so it's important not to rush this exercise.

Intervals

56

This exercise in sixths will really test your alternate-picking technique, so take your time and remember that rushing only leads to mistakes.

In order to apply alternate picking, your pick stroke will need to be much wider than normal. Here you can see the first down-pick skipping over the fifth string after playing the first note (C).

As you play the second note (A), your third and fourth fingers should already be in position above the ninth and tenth frets, ready to form the next sixth interval.

♩ 60–120

C major scale shape 1 – sixths

Note: You can transpose this exercise to other keys by starting on a different fret

In bar 2, the second sixth interval (C and A) can be played using the third and fourth fingers, as shown here. Although these notes are on the same fret, they are not on adjacent strings so fretting them both accurately with the fourth finger would be tricky.

However, the following sixth interval (beat 2, bar 2) can be played with finger rolling using your first finger, since these two notes both fall on the seventh fret.

57 Arpeggios

track 58

Diatonic arpeggios are constructed only from the notes of the parent scale, so they are an excellent resource for improvisation.

Use eighth-note triplet picking throughout, as indicated in bar 1. Remember that this will mean playing the first note on beat 2 (D) with an up-pick.

To shift smoothly from the last note (G) on beat 1 to the first note (D) on beat 2, use the finger-rolling technique applied with your fourth finger.

♩ 60–110

C major scale shape I – diatonic ascending triads

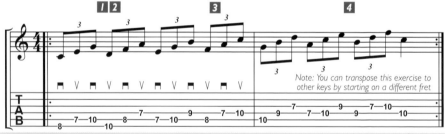

Note: You can transpose this exercise to other keys by starting on a different fret

When you're playing arpeggio patterns, you will be moving back and forth across the strings as you ascend, so make sure you keep your fingers in position above their respective frets at all times.

This photograph illustrates the finger-rolling technique being applied to the E and B notes in bar 2. Position your finger so that only the tip touches the fourth string as you fret the E, then as you roll the finger onto the fourth string it will simultaneously mute the third string.

Descending arpeggio patterns don't start on the root note but on the fifth of each triad – always think about the names of notes as you play.

Because the first note falls on the eighth fret, this should be played with your second finger. Notice how the third and fourth fingers are also in position above the ninth and tenth frets.

As soon as you've played the last note on beat 1 (C), roll your fourth finger onto the third string to play the F that quickly follows on beat 2.

♩ 60–110

C major scale shape I – diatonic descending triads

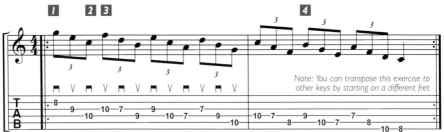

Note: You can transpose this exercise to other keys by starting on a different fret

Because these triplet patterns don't adhere to a specific string pattern, economy picking can only be partially used – you'll find it easier to use the alternate triplet picking shown. Here the first note on beat 2 is being played with an up-pick.

Remember to keep your fingers close to the strings, hovering above their respective frets. This photograph shows the B on beat 2 of bar 2 being fretted with the third finger, with the fourth and first fingers already in position and ready to play the remaining notes of the triad.

59 Arpeggios

○ track 60

Diatonic seventh arpeggios are four-note patterns and so lend themselves perfectly to 16th-note exercises like this one.

You'll be using all of your fretting-hand fingers in this exercise, so make sure your fingers are in position before you begin. Here you can see the second finger fretting the first note (C) while the first, third and fourth fingers hover above their respective frets.

Use the alternate 16th-note picking that is indicated on the first beat throughout the whole exercise. Here you can see the fourth note of bar 1 (B) being correctly played with an up-pick on the fourth string.

♩ 60–100

C major scale shape I – diatonic ascending 7th arpeggios

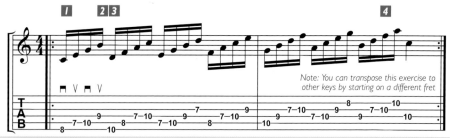

Note: You can transpose this exercise to other keys by starting on a different fret

The first note of beat 2 is on the tenth fret, so, as you play the final note on beat 1 (B), your fourth finger should be moving into position on the sixth string, as shown here.

In bar 2, the last three notes should be played using finger rolling with the fourth finger. It's important to prevent the notes from ringing into each other by applying finger pressure to only one string at a time.

track 61

Arpeggios

60

Descending seventh arpeggios don't start on the root note: they start on the seventh. This can be confusing so don't rush this exercise.

In order to apply the alternate picking indicated throughout, some of your pick strokes will traverse multiple strings. Here the pick is travelling back across the strings after playing the last up-pick on beat 1 to play the A on beat 2 with a down-pick.

At the same time, the fourth finger of your fretting hand will also need to roll off the fourth string and onto the second string as illustrated here.

♩ 60–100   C major scale shape I – diatonic descending 7th arpeggios

Note: You can transpose this exercise to other keys by starting on a different fret

Then, for the second note on beat 2, your fourth finger will need to roll again so that it frets only the third string, as this photograph illustrates.

The final arpeggio on beat 3 of bar 2 employs the fourth finger twice on the tenth fret. This time, instead of using finger rolling, you can reposition the fourth finger above the sixth string while playing the second note of the arpeggio (A).

61 Major-Key Chords

These invaluable major-key chord progressions can be used for chord practice and for scale and arpeggio workouts. By using the chord finder on page 115, you'll easily be able to transpose these sequences to any key.

61.1

61.2

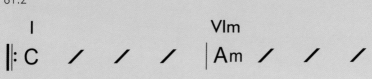

61.3

61.4

I ♭III

‖: C ╱ ╱ ╱ |E♭ ╱ ╱ ╱

IIm
| Dm / / / | / / / / :‖

IV   V
| F / / / | G / / / :‖

♭III   ♭VI
| E♭ / / / | A♭ / / / :‖

IV   IVm
| F / / / | Fm / / / :‖

61   Major-Key Chords cont.

61.5

I			II7		
‖: C△	╱	╱	╱	D7 ╱	╱ ╱

61.6

IV△	V7		I△	III7
‖: F△ ╱	G7 ╱		C△ ╱	E7 ╱

61.7

I△	IV△		VII∅	III7
‖: C△ ╱	F△ ╱		B∅ ╱	E7 ╱

61.8

I△	VI7		IIm7	V7
‖: C△ ╱	A7 ╱		Dm7 ╱	G7 ╱

61

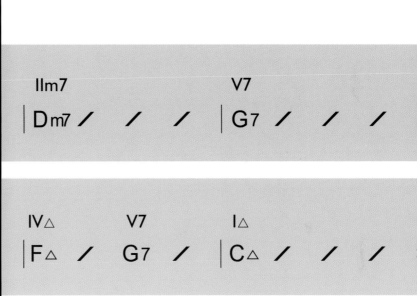

Minor-Key Chords

As with the major-key chords (see Exercise 61), you can use these minor-key chord progressions to practise your chords, scales and arpeggios. The chord finder on page 115 will help you to transpose these sequences to any key.

62.1

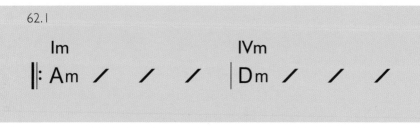

62.2

62.3

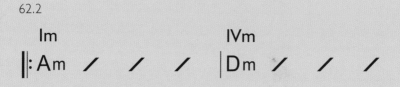

62.4

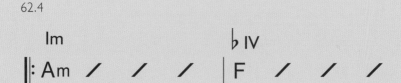

62

Im | V
Am / / / | E / / / :|

Vm | Im
Em / / / | Am / / / :|

♭IV | V
F / / / | E / / / :|

♭VII | Im
G / / / | Am / / / :|

62 Minor-Key Chords cont.

62.5

Im7			VIø		

‖: Am7 / / / | F#ø / / /

62.6

Im7			VIIm7	♭III7	

‖: Am7 / / / | Gm7 / C7 /

62.7

Im7	IV7	Im7	IV7

‖: Am7 / D7 / | Am7 / D7 /

62.8

IVm7	♭VII7	♭III△	♭VI△

‖: Dm7 / G7 / | C△ / F△ /

IIø   V7

| Bø / / / | E7 / / / :||

♭VI△   IIø   V7

| F△ / / / | Bø / E7 / :||

Im7   IV7   IIø   V7

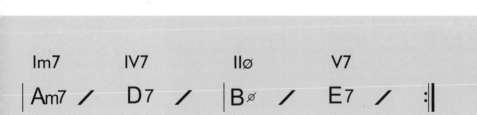

| Am7 / D7 / | Bø / E7 / :||

Im7   IV7   Im7   I7

| Bø / E7 / | Am7 / A7 / :||

63 Dominant-Seventh Chords

Dominant-seventh sequences are frequently used in jazz and blues. These genres have influenced just about every other style of popular music since the early 20th century. By using the chord finder on page 115 you'll easily be able to transpose these sequences to any key.

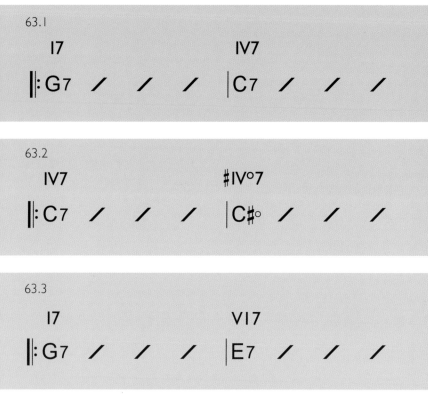

63.1

I7   IV7

‖: G7 ╱ ╱ ╱ |C7 ╱ ╱ ╱

63.2

IV7   ♯IV°7

‖: C7 ╱ ╱ ╱ |C♯° ╱ ╱ ╱

63.3

I7   VI7

‖: G7 ╱ ╱ ╱ |E7 ╱ ╱ ╱

63.4

I7   ♭III°7

‖: G7 ╱ ╱ ╱ |B♭° ╱ ╱ ╱

I7
| G7 / / / | D7 / / / :||

V7

I7
| G7 / / / | D7 / / / :||

V7

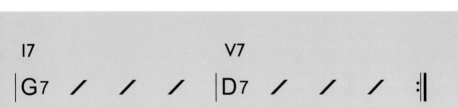

II7
| A7 / / / | D7 / / / :||

V7

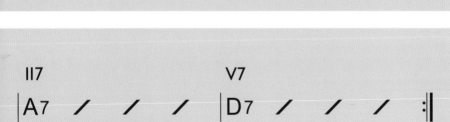

IIm7
| Am7 / / / | D7 / / / :||

V7

63.5

I7   III7

‖: G7 / / / | B♭7 / / /

63.6

IIm7   V7

‖: Am7 / / / | D7 / / /

63.7

I7   VI7   II7   V7

‖: G7 / E7 / | A7 / D7 /

63.8

I7   VI7   III7   VI7

‖: G7 / C7 / | B7 / E7 /

II7   ♭II7

| A7 / / / | A♭7 / / / :‖

I7   ♭III7   ♭VI7   ♭II7

| G7 / B♭7 / | E♭7 / A♭7 / :‖

IIIø   VI7   II7   V7

| Bø / E7 / | A7 / D7 / :‖

II7   V7   ♭VIm7   ♭II7

| A7 / D7 / | E♭m7 / A♭7 / :‖

The
Workouts

Chapter 2

Rhythm Guitar

TIME	EXERCISE	CHORDS & SCALES	NOTES
1 min	Prep	Chords: G (p. 130), D (p. 120), Am (p. 134)	Review these chords, then warm up by changing quickly and smoothly between each shape. **Tip**: Use your first, second and third fingers to fret the G shape.
1 min	61.1 (p. 76–77)	G, D, Am	You'll need to transpose this sequence to the key of G, but don't panic! All you need to do is substitute G, D, Am instead of playing the chords C, G, Dm as written. Use the chord finder on p. 115 to verify.
2 mins	1 (p. 16)	G, D, Am	This easy half-note rhythm pattern allows you to focus on your fretting hand. Let the chords ring for their full value; don't cheat by cutting them short! Start at 70bpm, building tempo gradually over several sessions.
2 mins	2 (p. 17)	G, D, Am	This rhythm pattern adds a quarter-note strum on the second beat of each bar. You'll still have plenty of time to change chords, but make sure you add the ghosted down-strum on the fourth beat.
4 mins	3 (p. 18)	G, D, Am	To round off the workout, add in the quarter-note strum on beat 4 where you previously played a ghosted down-strum. This sequence should now start to sound familiar! It's a Bob Dylan tune that was famously covered by Eric Clapton and Guns n' Roses.

TIME	EXERCISE	CHORDS & SCALES	NOTES
1 min	Prep	Chords: Em (p. 124), Am (p. 134), B7 (p. 138)	Practise moving quickly between the chords, keeping your fingers close to the fingerboard. **Tip**: To change smoothly from Em to B7 (and vice versa), try keeping your second finger on the fingerboard.
1 min	62.1 (p. 80–81)	Em, Am, B7	Ignore the written chords and transpose this sequence to Em (using the chord finder on p. 115 if you wish). This will enable you to apply the chords you prepped above to the sequence.
2 mins	1 (p. 16)	Em, Am, B7	This half-note rhythm pattern leaves plenty of time for chord changes. Remember that it's important to practise with a metronome, ideally at around 70–80bpm to start.
3 mins	4 (p. 19)	Em, Am, B7	This two-bar rhythm pattern will need to be repeated to fit into your four-bar sequence. You should end up with half notes in bars 1 and 3, and quarter notes in bars 2 and 4.
3 mins	3 (p. 18)	Em, Am, B7	This pattern adds a quarter-note strum throughout the sequence, so you will have less time to change chords. Make sure you practise with a metronome and start slowly at no more than 70bpm.

TIME	EXERCISE	CHORDS & SCALES	NOTES
1 min	Prep	Chords: G7 (p. 131), E7 (p. 125), A7 (p. 135), D7 (p. 121)	Review these shapes carefully. Check your barring technique is solid by making sure that all the notes are ringing clearly, adjusting your hand position if necessary (ensure your thumb is always behind the neck, supporting your first finger).
1 min	63.3 (p. 84–85)	G7, E7, A7, D7	Run through the sequence without the metronome to familiarise yourself with the changes. **Tip:** When shifting shapes, just release the pressure of your first finger barre, but don't remove it from the strings completely.
2 mins	3 (p. 18)	G7, E7, A7, D7	This simple quarter-note rhythm uses a down-strum pattern throughout. This will allow you to focus entirely on your fretting hand. Start at around 90bpm, building up to 120bpm gradually over several sessions.
2 mins	6 (p. 21)	G7, E7, A7, D7	Remember that you can change chords on the last up-strum when you're playing eighth-note rhythms. You'll be strumming the open strings and moving your fretting-hand fingers simultaneously. Start slowly at 60bpm.
4 mins	8 (p. 23)	G7, E7, A7, D7	This rhythm pattern adds a tie between the second and third beats to create syncopation. Make sure your strumming arm is moving exactly the same as in the previous pattern, adding a ghosted down-strum on beat 3.

TIME	EXERCISE	CHORDS & SCALES	NOTES
1 min	Prep	Chords: F△ (p. 142), G7 (p. 131), C△ (p. 142), E7 (p. 124)	Get up to speed on your major-seventh chords with this jazzy-sounding sequence. **Tip:** Use F△ shape 1 and C△ shape 4. You can find these moveable chord forms on p. 142 and 143.
1 min	61.6 (p. 78–79)	F△, G7, C△, E7	Although there are only four chords in this sequence, you'll be mixing them with barre forms, so you'll need to make swift (and accurate) position shifts when changing shapes.
2 mins	1 (p. 16)	F△, G7, C△, E7	Although this is a half-note rhythm pattern, you'll still need to change chords on every strum (except in bar 4). Practise slowly at first (70–80bpm), increasing the tempo only once you've achieved accuracy.
2 mins	3 (p. 18)	F△, G7, C△, E7	This constant quarter-note rhythm pattern will ensure your chord changes are slick and efficient. Don't forget that metronome! Start at 70bpm.
4 mins	8 (p. 23)	F△, G7, C△, E7	This pattern adds a tie on beat 2 so you'll need to 'push' in the second chord of each bar (i.e. by playing it on '2+'). **Tip:** Minimise finger movement when changing shapes by sliding them along the strings to their new position.

RHYTHM GUITAR ▷ Intermediate 1

RHYTHM GUITAR ▷ Intermediate 2

RHYTHM GUITAR ▷ Pro 1

TIME	EXERCISE	CHORDS & SCALES	NOTES
1 min	Prep	Chords: Am7 (p. 144–145), D9 (p. 146–147), Dm (p. 121), G#° (p. 149)	Use moveable shapes with the root on the fifth string for Am7 and D9. The G#° should be played with its root on the fourth string.
1 min	62.7 (p. 82–83)	Am7, D9, Dm, G#°	We'll be substituting D9 for the D7 in this sequence and using Dm and G#° to generate 'top string voicings' for B and E7 respectively. By using a diminished voicing for E7 you will actually be playing E79.
2 mins	8 (p. 23)	Am7, D9, Dm, G#°	Play this syncopated eighth-note pattern at 120bpm to achieve an authentic Latin flavour, reminiscent of Santana's early work.
2 mins	9 (p. 24)	Am7, D9, Dm, G#°	This rhythm pattern generates a cool reggae-style vamp that sounds best when played with swing 16th notes between 65 and 75bpm. **Tip:** Release the pressure of your fretting hand between strums to keep the notes short.
4 mins	12 (p. 27)	Am7, D9, Dm, G#°	Instead of playing one chord per bar as written, change chords on the offbeat of beat 2 to allow this rhythm to fit your 'two-chords-per-bar' sequence. This funky, slick groove works best between 80 and 90bpm.

RHYTHM GUITAR ▷ Pro 2

TIME	EXERCISE	CHORDS & SCALES	NOTES
1 min	Prep	Chords: G7 (p. 131), C7 (p. 117), B7 (p. 139), E7 (p. 125)	Use moveable forms throughout (as suggested in library pages) to ensure quick changes and avoid having to mute unwanted open strings. To change quickly from G7 to C7, release the pressure of your fretting hand and slide the shape (intact) to the eighth fret.
1 min	Prep	A7 (p. 135), D7 (p. 121), E♭m7 (p. 145), A♭7 (p. 132)	Always look for shortcuts that will help to minimise finger movement when changing shapes. To move from D7 to E♭m7, slide the shape up one fret and remove your fourth finger while adding the second.
2 mins	63.8 (p. 86–87)	G7, C7, B7, E7, A7, D7, E♭m7, A♭7	There are a lot of chords here so begin by playing through this sequence out of time (i.e. without the metronome), keeping all fretting-hand finger movements as slight as possible.
3 mins	1 (p. 16)	G7, C7, B7, E7, A7, D7, E♭m7, A♭7	To ensure all your changes are accurate you need to first practise the sequence with this half-note rhythm. Allow each chord to ring for its full value (no cheating!). Start at 120bpm.
3 mins	3 (p. 18)	G7, C7, B7, E7, A7, D7, E♭m7, A♭7	This constant quarter-note rhythm pattern will allow you to achieve a cool, jazzy composition. Ultimately, you should be able to play this at 200–220bpm. **Tip:** For an authentic Wes Montgomery style, ditch the pick and use your thumb!

Fingerpicking

TIME	EXERCISE	CHORDS & SCALES	NOTES
1 min	Prep	Chords: Em (p. 124), G (p. 130)	Review both of these shapes. Fret the G chord using your second and third fingers only. Since you won't be playing the first string, you'll be able to change chords more quickly if you don't fret it.
1 min	Prep	C (p. 116), B7 (p. 138)	One of the great things about fingerpicking is that you can always omit fingers for strings you won't be playing. So you can omit your fourth finger when forming the B7 shape.
2 mins	62.3 (p. 80–81)	Em, G, C, B7	You'll need to transpose this sequence to the key of Em. Do this using the chord finder on p. 115. You should end up with this sequence: Em, G, C, B7 (change the last chord from V to V7).
2 mins	13 (p. 28)	Em, G, C, B7	You'll need to move your thumb across the strings so that it picks the fifth and fourth strings in bars 3 and 4 (m and i pick the same strings as before). **Tip**: Pick each string with equal 'weight' to allow both bass and melody to be heard.
4 mins	13 (p. 28)	Em, G, C, B7	Now you can make this pattern more challenging by separating the bass and melody notes; this creates syncopation. In bar 1, pick the bass note (E) on the sixth string, and then play the melody note (B) on beat 2. Apply this approach to the rest of the sequence.

TIME	EXERCISE	CHORDS & SCALES	NOTES
1 min	Prep	Chords: C (p. 116), Am (p. 134)	Don't fingerpick the chords yet, just strum each once so you can focus on your fretting hand. Keep your first and second fingers in position when changing – they don't need to move.
1 min	Prep	F (p. 126), G (p. 130)	The G can be played using only your second and third fingers (omit the first string), so focus on that tricky full F barre shape. Check that all six strings are ringing clearly, adjusting your fingers/hand position if needed.
2 mins	61.2 (p. 76–77)	C, Am, F, G	Just strum this sequence through to make sure you are comfortable with the shapes and there are no hesitations between changes.
3 mins	15 (p. 30)	C, Am, F, G	You'll need to switch the bass note pattern in bars 3 and 4 to accommodate the sixth-string root chords, F and G. To do this, start with your thumb on the sixth string (simultaneously pinching the chord notes) then play the fifth string on the second beat.
3 mins	16 (p. 31)	C, Am, F, G	Modify the bass pattern, as before, in bars 3 and 4. This will allow you to apply this classic country-style picking pattern to the whole sequence. **Tip**: Lightly rest the palm of your picking hand on the bass strings to achieve a tighter, more percussive performance.

TIME	EXERCISE	CHORDS & SCALES	NOTES
1 min	Prep	Chords: C (p. 117), Am (p. 134), F (p. 126), G (p. 130)	You'll probably want to spend most of this time reviewing that full F barre shape. It's important to ensure that each string is clearly ringing. Adjust your hand/finger positions as necessary.
1 min	61.2 (p. 76–77)	C, Am, F, G	Run through the sequence (without the metronome) to familiarise yourself with the changes. **Tip:** Keep your fourth finger hovering close to the strings while playing Am: this will speed up your change to the F.
2 mins	17 (p. 32)	C, Am, F, G	This classic 6/8 picking pattern sounds great when applied to the previous sequence. Repeat bar 1 of the picking pattern for the first two bars of the sequence, and bar 2 for bars 3 and 4 (to keep the thumb on the correct strings for the bass notes).
2 mins	18 (p. 33)	C, Am, F, G	In bars 3 and 4, you will need to move your thumb onto the sixth string to play the correct bass notes (keep the rest of the pattern as is). The top note should be repeated for the F chord, but you could play G on beat 1 and F on beat 3 of the final bar (G–G7).
4 mins	19 (p. 34)	C, Am, F, G	As in the previous picking pattern, move your thumb onto the sixth string in bars 3 and 4 of this sequence. Some fingerpickers like to play the F without barring (i.e. by fretting the sixth string with their thumb). This works fine when you're not playing all six strings as in this pattern.

TIME	EXERCISE	CHORDS & SCALES	NOTES
1 min	Prep	Chords: D7 (C7 p. 116 – moved up 2 frets), G7 (p. 130)	Instead of playing an open D7, use the moveable shape 3 version of this chord. To do this, form the open C7 shape (p. 116) and slide it two frets higher so that your first finger is now on the third fret.
1 min	Prep	E7 (C7 p. 116 – move up 4 frets), A7 (p. 135)	You'll need to use the moveable C7 shape for the E7 chord, too (with your first finger on the fifth fret, second string). Keep your third finger in position when changing to A7.
1 min	63.3 (p. 84–85)	G7, E7, D7, A7	Practise the chord sequence without a metronome by simply strumming each chord once (using your thumb), then changing. Your third finger remains on the fifth string throughout so don't take it off the string.
3 mins	20 (p. 35)	G7, E7, D7, A7	Practise this sequence by picking out only the bass notes to start. Use bar 2 of the picking pattern for G7 and A7, and bar 1 for E7 and D7. Make sure you form the full chord shape, and use your *i*, *m* and *a* fingers to pinch the chord notes on the first beat only.
4 mins	20 (p. 35)	G7, E7, D7, A7	Once you can play the bass notes without mistakes, you can start adding the melody notes to achieve the full picking pattern. **Tip:** Add the notes one at a time, repeating the sequence to eliminate errors.

TIME	EXERCISE	CHORDS & SCALES	NOTES
1 min	Prep	Chords: Dm7 (p. 144–145), G7 (p. 131), C△, F△ (p. 142)	Use moveable shapes with the root on the fifth string for Dm7 and C△. The F△ can be played open with its root on the fourth string. For G7, use a regular, shape 1 full barre chord.
1 min	(Prep)	Bø (p. 148–149), E7 (p. 124), Am7 (p. 144–145), A7 (p. 134)	Use the moveable shape 4 version of Bø. The remaining chords can be played in open position. **Tip:** Keep your fourth finger in position when changing from Bø to E7.
2 mins	62.8 (p. 82–83)	Dm7, G7, C△, F△, Bø, E7, Am7, A7	Play through this sequence without a metronome, strumming each chord once with your thumb. Aim to minimise all your finger movements when changing shapes, as this will facilitate quick changes.
3 mins	22 (p. 37)	Dm7, G7, C△, F△, Bø, E7, Am7, A7	Use the picking given for C in the exercise when playing Dm7, C△, Bø, Am7 and A7 (i.e. fifth-string root pattern); use the Dm7 picking (fourth-string root pattern) for F△; and finally use the Dm7/G picking for G7 and E7 (sixth-string root pattern).
3 mins	23 (p. 38)	Dm7, G7, C△, F△, Bø, E7, Am7, A7	Adjust the picking pattern for sixth-string root chords (G7 and E7) by moving your thumb onto the sixth string. You'll also need to adapt it slightly to play F△: use the picking pattern given in bar 1 and move all your fingers one set of strings higher, so your thumb starts on the fourth string and *i*, *m* and *a* pick the top three strings.

TIME	EXERCISE	CHORDS & SCALES	NOTES
1 min	Prep	Chords: G7 (p. 131), E7 (p. 124), A7 (p. 134), D7 (p. 116), Bø (p. 148–149)	Use the open C7 (shape 3) played two frets higher for D7. Use the same fingering given for C7 on p. 116. Use the moveable form for Bø, with the root on the fifth string.
1 min	63.7 (p. 86–87)	G7, E7, A7, D7, Bø	Play through this sequence without a metronome, strumming each chord once only with your thumb. This will enable you to check that economy of movement is being applied to every change.
2 mins	24 (p. 39)	G, C/G (p. 39)	Play this exercise with the chords indicated so you can focus on your picking hand. **Tip:** You'll find it much easier to learn this pattern if you start with the bass notes and add the melody one note at a time.
2 mins	63.7 (p. 86–87)	G7, E7, A7, D7, Bø	Practise the sequence adding only the bass notes, using the picking pattern from Exercise 24 (above). Remember to start with your thumb picking the fifth string for E7, D7 and Bø (don't alter the upper bass note, as this is still played on the fourth string).
4 mins	24 (p. 39)	G7, E7, A7, D7, Bø	Once you're happy with the bassline and you can play it accurately and confidently, start adding melody notes. Picking patterns with a strong bass part often sound best with the bass strings lightly palm-muted.

Alternate Picking

TIME	EXERCISE	CHORDS & SCALES	NOTES
1 min	25 (p. 40)		Warm up with this exercise. Be sure to use all four fingers of your fretting hand, starting with your first. 'Anchor' your picking hand by resting your third and/or fourth fingers on the guitar's pickguard or body.
1 min	Prep	Scale: A minor pentatonic shape 1 (p. 152)	If you don't know this shape already, learn it thoroughly before continuing. This 1 minute is for prep only (i.e. refreshing your memory). Practise ascending and descending without a metronome, taking care to follow the indicated fingering.
2 mins	27 (p. 42)	A minor pentatonic shape 1	This exercise demonstrates how to play the lower octave (starting on the sixth string, fifth fret) using alternate picking. Always keep your pick at 90° to the strings.
2 mins	27 (p. 42)	A minor pentatonic shape 1	Practise the upper octave (i.e. from the seventh fret on the fourth string), using the shape 1 pattern on p. 152 to guide you. The final note should be a quarter note as before. Repeat the pattern several times.
4 mins	27 (p. 42)	A minor pentatonic shape 1	To complete your workout, practise the full two-octave scale using eighth-note alternate picking. It should take three bars to complete (ascending and descending). Make your last note (A on the sixth string) a quarter note so that repeats start on beat 1. **Tip**: Use a metronome, beginning your practice slowly at 70bpm.

TIME	EXERCISE	CHORDS & SCALES	NOTES
1 min	26 (p. 41)		Use this exercise as a picking-hand warm-up. Make sure you use finger rolling as advised in the text. As you flatten your finger across the higher string, the tip of your finger should roll off the lower string so that your fingertip mutes it.
1 min	Prep	Scale: C major shape 1 (p. 176)	If this scale is unfamiliar to you, take some time out to learn it thoroughly before proceeding. Whether you're prepping or learning, use the fingering indicated.
2 mins	28 (p. 43)	C major shape 1	This exercise demonstrates how to play the lower octave (starting on the sixth string, eighth fret) using alternate picking. **Tip**: Keep your fingers hovering close to the strings when not fretting.
2 mins	28 (p. 43)	C major shape 1	Work on the upper octave (from the tenth fret on the fourth string) using the shape 1 pattern on p. 176 as reference. The final note should be a quarter note as before. Repeat several times.
4 mins	28 (p. 43)	C major shape 1	Play the full two-octave scale using eighth-note alternate picking. It will take three bars to complete (ascending and descending). Make your last note (C on the sixth string) a quarter note so that the sequence repeats from beat 1. Don't rush (tempo should be 60–70bpm to start).

TIME	EXERCISE	CHORDS & SCALES	NOTES
2 mins	Prep	Scale: A minor pentatonic shapes 2–5 (p. 152–153)	If you don't know these shapes you'll need to spend a bit of time learning them thoroughly before continuing. Practise each ascending and descending, taking care to follow the fingering indicated.
2 mins	31 (p. 46)	A minor pentatonic shapes 1 and 2 (p. 152)	Run through the exercise once as written, then apply shape 2 of the A minor pentatonic scale using exactly the same string and picking pattern (i.e. beginning on the sixth string). Shape 2 should begin with your second finger on the eighth fret.
2 mins	31 (p. 46)	A minor pentatonic shape 3	You can adapt the exercise to work with shape 3 of the scale. Shape 3 should start with your first finger on the tenth fret. Remember to use alternate picking throughout!
2 mins	31 (p. 46)	A minor pentatonic shape 4	Now you can apply the practice sequence to shape 4 of the A minor pentatonic. The pattern should start with your first finger on the twelfth fret. **Tip:** You can also play shape 4 in open position.
2 mins	31 (p. 46)	A minor pentatonic shape 5	You can easily use this exercise with shape 5 of the scale. Use exactly the same string and picking pattern (i.e. beginning on the sixth string). The pattern should start with your first finger on the third fret.

TIME	EXERCISE	CHORDS & SCALES	NOTES
2 mins	Prep	Scale: C major shapes 2–5 (p. 176–177)	If you're not comfortable with these shapes, spend a few sessions learning them before continuing. Practise each shape ascending and descending, taking care to follow the fingering indicated.
2 mins	36 (p. 51)	C major shapes 1 and 2 (p. 176)	Run through the exercise once as written. Then apply the same ascending/descending pattern to shape 2 of the C major scale. Start the scale on the second note (with your third finger on the twelfth fret) to maintain the same sequencing pattern. Keep the tempo easy at around 60bpm.
2 mins	36 (p. 51)	C major shape 3	Adapt the exercise to work with shape 3 of the scale. Use the same string and picking pattern (i.e. beginning on the sixth string). Start the scale on the second note (with your second finger on the thirteenth fret).
2 mins	36 (p. 51)	C major shape 4	By now the routine should be familiar, so you'll have no problem applying the sequence to shape 4. Start the scale on the lowest note (i.e. with your second finger on the third fret). For the last note, play an F on the first fret with your first finger.
2 mins	36 (p. 51)	C major shape 5	Finally you can apply the pattern to shape 5 of the scale. Start the scale on the second note (i.e. with your third finger on the seventh fret). Practise this invaluable workout in as many different keys as you can.

ALTERNATE PICKING △ Pro 1

TIME	EXERCISE	CHORDS & SCALES	NOTES
1 min	33 (p. 48)		This exercise makes an ideal warm-up. Build to the upper tempo range (100bpm), keeping your picking even and consistent. **Tip**: Accent the first note in each 16th-note grouping to achieve ultimate pick control.
2 mins	Prep	Scale: A minor pentatonic shapes 1–5 (p. 152–153)	Warm up by practising the scales in sequence. You don't need to use a metronome at this point, but make sure you're using the fingering indicated. Practise each shape ascending and descending.
1 min	35 (p. 50)	A minor pentatonic shape 1	Run through the exercise, taking care to observe the 16th-note picking throughout. Note that there are always two notes on each string except when descending (where only one note is played on the first string). Remember to set your metronome to 3/4!
3 mins	35 (p. 50)	A minor pentatonic shapes 2 and 3	You can easily adapt Exercise 35 to work with shapes 2 and 3. Use the same string and picking pattern (beginning on the sixth string and lowest scale note). The last note of both shapes should be played as an eighth note (as above).
3 mins	35 (p. 50)	A minor pentatonic shapes 4 and 5	To round off this workout, adapt the exercise to work with shapes 4 and 5. Use exactly the same string and picking pattern (i.e. beginning on the sixth string and lowest scale note) and play the last note of both shapes as an eighth note (as above).

ALTERNATE PICKING △ Pro 2

TIME	EXERCISE	CHORDS & SCALES	NOTES
1 min	34 (p. 49)		Warm up your fingers with this exercise, building to the upper tempo of 100bpm. Keep your picking even and consistent and accent the first note in each 16th-note grouping to enhance your control.
2 mins	Prep	Scale: C major shapes 1–5 (p. 176–177)	Run through the scales in sequence, making sure to practise each shape ascending and descending. You don't need to use a metronome, but make sure you use the indicated fingering.
1 min	36 (p. 51)	C major shape 1	Practise the exercise, observing the 16th-note picking indicated. Use the fingering given on p. 176 in the scale library. You should aim to play this at the upper tempo (100bpm).
3 mins	36 (p. 51)	C major shapes 2 and 3	Adapt the exercise to work with shapes 2 and 3 of the C major scale. Use the same string and picking pattern (i.e. beginning on the sixth string). Begin shape 2 with your third finger (twelfth fret) and shape 3 with your second finger (thirteenth fret).
3 mins	36 (p. 51)	C major shapes 4 and 5	You can also adapt the exercise to work with shapes 4 and 5. Use exactly the same string and picking pattern (i.e. beginning on the sixth string). Start shape 4 with your second finger (third fret), adding the last note (F) on the first fret. Start shape 5 with your third finger (seventh fret).

Legato

TIME	EXERCISE	CHORDS & SCALES	NOTES
1 min	Prep		Warm up by hammering your third finger onto any fret after picking any open string (e.g. pick the sixth string and hammer-on to the third fret). Do this across all six strings or just focusing on the lower or higher strings.
1 min	Prep	Scale: G minor pentatonic shape 1 (p. 172)	If you don't know this shape, learn it thoroughly before continuing. The minute timeframe is purely for refreshing your memory. Practise ascending and descending (using down-picks for each note) making sure you use the suggested fingering.
2 mins	38 (p. 53)	G minor pentatonic shape 1	This exercise demonstrates how to practise ascending and descending hammer-ons using the lower octave of the pentatonic shape. Hammer your fingers firmly onto the strings immediately behind the frets.
2 mins		G minor pentatonic shape 1	Practise hammer-ons using the upper octave of the pentatonic shape (i.e. on the top three strings). You can ascend and descend across the strings or use the same pattern as above (but starting on the third string).
4 mins		G minor pentatonic shape 1	Practise the full two-octave scale using hammer-ons. Ascend all six strings (pausing on the final note to allow it to ring to the end of the bar), and then descend all six strings, hammering onto the second note of each string. Use a metronome and begin your practice slowly at 60bpm.

TIME	EXERCISE	CHORDS & SCALES	NOTES
1 min	Prep		Start by pulling-off from any fretted note to an open string, using your third finger (e.g. pick the sixth string and pull-off from the third fret). You can do this across all six strings or focus on the lower or higher strings.
1 min	Prep	Scale: G minor pentatonic shape 1 (p. 172)	Use this 1 minute for prep only. Make sure you learn this shape thoroughly before continuing. Practise ascending and descending (using down-picks to play each note), making sure you use the fingering given.
2 mins	42 (p. 57)	G minor pentatonic shape 1	In this exercise you will practise ascending and descending pull-offs using the lower octave of the pentatonic shape. **Tip:** Flick your finger sideways as you release it from the string to generate a clear lower note.
2 mins		G minor pentatonic shape 1	Practise pull-offs using the upper octave of the pentatonic shape (i.e. on the top three strings). You can use the same ascending and descending pattern as above (but starting on the third string) or simply ascend and descend across the strings.
4 mins		G minor pentatonic shape 1	Beginning slowly at 60bpm, work through the full two-octave scale using pull-offs. Ascend all six strings (pausing on the final note to allow it to ring to the end of the bar), then descend all six strings, pulling off to the lower note on each string.

LEGATO △ Intermediate 1

TIME	EXERCISE	CHORDS & SCALES	NOTES
1 min	Prep	Scale: C major shapes 1 and 4 (p. 176–177)	If you don't know these shapes, study them thoroughly before continuing. This 1 minute is intended for prep only. Practise ascending and descending (using down-picks for each note), making sure you use the fingering given.
1 min	39 (p. 54)	C major shape 1	Practise ascending the scale by picking only the first note on each string. Hammer your fingers firmly onto the strings close behind the frets.
1 min	43 (p. 58)	C major shape 1	Use this exercise to practise descending the scale, picking the first note on each string only. **Tip**: Flick your fingers sideways as you release them to generate clear lower notes.
3 mins	39 (p. 54) and 43 (p. 58)	C major shape 1	Practise ascending and descending the full two-octave shape by combining the previous two examples. Remember to pause before descending or repeating (the last note is always a quarter note). Start slowly at 80bpm: it's important not to rush this exercise.
4 mins	39 (p. 54) and 43 (p. 58)	C major shape 4	Because this shape contains an extra note on the second string, you can play the notes on the first string (G and A) using consecutive hammer-on/pull-offs (without pausing). The sequence takes four bars to complete. Pause on the last note (by playing a quarter note) before repeating.

LEGATO △ Intermediate 2

TIME	EXERCISE	CHORDS & SCALES	NOTES
1 min	Prep	Scale: G major shapes 2 and 5 (p. 190–191)	You'll be using these two patterns to play A Dorian mode shapes 1 and 4 (major shape 2 = Dorian shape 1; major shape 5 = Dorian shape 4). Use the mode finder on p. 151 to verify the location of root notes.
1 min	39 (p. 54)	A Dorian mode shape 1	Use the hammer-on concept illustrated in this exercise and apply it to shape 1 of the Dorian mode. Apply three-notes-per-string hammer-ons where necessary.
1 min	43 (p. 58)	A Dorian mode shape 1	Use the pull-off technique in this exercise and apply it to shape 1 of the Dorian mode. Apply three-note-per-string pull-offs where needed.
3 mins	39 (p. 54) and 43 (p. 58)	A Dorian mode shape 1	Combine the previous two exercises and practise ascending and descending the full two-octave shape. Play only two notes on the highest string, using a consecutive hammer-on/pull-off. This will allow the sequence to fit in a four-bar repeating cycle.
4 mins	39 (p. 54) and 43 (p. 58)	A Dorian mode shape 4	Now practise ascending and descending shape 4 of the same mode, applying legato technique throughout. Play only two notes on the highest string, using a consecutive hammer-on/pull-off so that the sequence fits in a four-bar repeating cycle.

TIME	EXERCISE	CHORDS & SCALES	NOTES
3 mins	Prep	Scale: A minor pentatonic shapes 1–3 (p. 152–153)	Revise these three shapes by playing them quickly in sequence. Use alternate 16th-note picking so you can concentrate on applying minimal fretting-hand movement. Use a metronome set between 100–120bpm.
2 mins	Prep	A minor pentatonic shapes 4 and 5 (p. 153)	Apply the same routine as above to these two shapes, repeating each pattern and applying alternate picking throughout.
1 min	46 (p. 61)	A minor pentatonic shape 1	This exercise demonstrates how to practise the minor pentatonic by picking only the first note on each string. **Tip:** Try playing this in 3/4 to eliminate the quarter notes.
2 mins		A minor pentatonic shapes 2 and 3	Apply the legato technique to shapes 2 and 3 of the minor pentatonic. Play them in 3/4 time and omit the tied quarter note on beat 4 of the original exercise (46). Accent the first note in each group of 16ths to achieve ultimate pick control.
2 mins		A minor pentatonic shapes 4 and 5	To finish, apply the legato technique to shapes 4 and 5 of the scale. As above, play them in 3/4 time and omit the tied quarter note on beat 4 of Exercise 46. Keep your fingers close to the fingerboard at all times to minimise muscle fatigue.

TIME	EXERCISE	CHORDS & SCALES	NOTES
3 mins	Prep	Scale: C major shapes 1–3 (p. 176–177)	Play these shapes quickly in sequence to warm up (use a metronome at about 100–120bmp). Using alternate 16th-note picking will allow you to concentrate on keeping fretting-hand movement to a minimum.
2 mins	Prep	C major shapes 4 and 5 (p. 177)	Repeat the above routine with shapes 4 and 5. Run through each a few times and apply alternate picking throughout.
1 min	46 (p. 61)	C major shapes 1 and 2	Shapes 1 and 2 of the major scale have been combined in this exercise to create a true three-notes-per-string pattern. It's crucial that your fretting fingers are above their respective frets before you pick the first note.
2 mins		C major shapes 2–4	Combine shapes 2 and 3 then 3 and 4 to create two more three-notes-per-string patterns. Apply the legato technique ascending and descending. Set your metronome to 5/4 to allow the first-string notes to be included in your workout.
2 mins		C major shapes 1, 4 and 5	Next combine shapes 4 and 5 then 5 and 1 to create the final two three-note patterns. Apply the legato technique ascending and descending. Set your metronome to 5/4 so that the first-string notes are included.

Chord Master

TIME	EXERCISE	CHORDS & SCALES	NOTES
2 mins	62.4 (p. 80–81)	Chords: Am (p. 134), F (p. 126), G (p. 130)	Review the chords if necessary then play through the sequence using a basic one-strum-per-beat rhythm (i.e. four down-strums per bar). Use your second, third and fourth fingers to fret the G chord.
2 mins	Prep	Em (p. 124), C (p. 116), D (p. 120)	Transpose this sequence to the key of Em (cover up the chord column to test your transposing skills). Use the chord finder on p. 115 to verify.
2 mins	62.4 (p. 80–81)	Em, C, D	Run through the sequence in the new key, following the roman numerals above the chord symbols. This will help you to think harmonically when you see a chord progression. You will eventually be able to recognise common sequences at sight.
2 mins	Prep	Dm (p. 120), B♭ (p. 136), C	Now transpose the sequence to the key of Dm (hide the chord column to test your skills). You can use the chord finder on p. 115 to help.
2 mins	62.4 (p. 80–81)	Dm, B♭, C	To complete the workout, play through the sequence while thinking about each chord's harmonic function, e.g. Dm=Im, B♭=♭VIm, C=♭VIIm. **Tip**: Use your third finger to barre the third fret when playing B♭, angling your finger at the first knuckle to keep the first string muted.

TIME	EXERCISE	CHORDS & SCALES	NOTES
2 mins	63.1 (p. 84–85)	Chords: G7 (p. 130), C7 (p. 116), D7 (p. 120)	Revise chords if necessary then play the sequence using a one-strum-per-beat rhythm (i.e. four down-strums per bar). I7, IV7 and V7 are very important: they're the chords used in a 12-bar blues.
2 mins	Prep	A7 (p. 134), D7, E7 (p. 124)	Using the chord finder on p. 115 to help, transpose this sequence to the key of A. Cover up the chord column if you want to test yourself.
2 mins	63.1 (p. 84–85)	A7, D7, E7	Play the sequence in the new key, following the roman numerals above the chord symbols. By learning to think harmonically when you see a chord progression, you will eventually be able to instantly recognise common sequences.
2 mins	Prep	E7, A7, B7 (p. 138)	Covering up the chord column if you want, transpose this sequence to the key of E, using the chord finder on p. 115 to verify.
2 mins	63.1 (p. 84–85)	E7, A7, B7	As you play through the sequence, think of each chord in Nashville numbering, e.g. E7=I7, A7=IV7, B7=V7. **Tip**: Keep your second and third fingers at 90° to the fingerboard to avoid inadvertently damping higher strings.

TIME	EXERCISE	CHORDS & SCALES	NOTES
2 mins	61.4 (p. 76–77)	Chords: C (p. 117), E♭ (p. 123), F, Fm (p. 127)	Play the C as a shape 1 barre chord, and the E♭, F and Fm as shape 4 barre chords. Angle your third finger at the first knuckle to keep the first string muted when playing E♭ and F.
2 mins	Prep	F (p. 126), A♭ (p. 132), B♭, B♭m (p. 137)	Transpose the above sequence to the key of F (cover up the chord column to test your transposing skills). You can use the chord finder on p. 115 to verify. Use shape 1 barre forms for all four chords.
2 mins	61.4 (p. 76–77)	F, A♭, B♭, B♭m	Following the roman numerals above the chord symbols, work through the sequence in the new key. This will help you to think harmonically when you see a chord progression and eventually you'll be able to recognise common sequences easily.
2 mins	Prep	B♭, D♭ (p. 119), E♭, E♭m (p. 123)	Transpose this sequence to the key of B♭ using the chord finder on p. 115. Use shape 1 barre chords for B♭ and D♭, and shape 4 barre chords for E♭ and E♭m.
2 mins	61.4 (p. 76–77)	B♭, D♭, E♭, E♭m	Play the sequence while thinking of the chords by their Nashville numbering steps in the key of B♭ (i.e. I, ♭III, IV and IVm). This will ultimately enable you to transpose any progression at sight.

TIME	EXERCISE	CHORDS & SCALES	NOTES
2 mins	63.3 (p. 84–85)	Chords: G7 (p. 131), E7 (p. 125), A7 (p. 135), D7 (p. 121)	Play the G7 and A7 as shape 1 barre chords, and the E7 and D7 as shape 4 barre chords. Keep your third finger at right angles to the string when playing E7 and D7 to avoid inadvertently muting the third string.
2 mins	Prep	E♭7 (p. 123), C7 (p. 117), F7 (p. 127), B♭7 (p. 137)	Transpose this sequence to the key of E♭. Cover the chord column to test your transposing skills and use the chord finder on p. 115 to check. Use shape 4 barres for E♭7 and F7, and shape 1 barres for C7 and B♭7.
2 mins	61.4 (p. 76–77)	E♭7, C7, F7, B♭7	Practise the sequence in the new key, following the numerals above the chord symbols. Doing this will train you to think harmonically when you see a chord progression and you will soon be able to recognise common sequences at sight.
2 mins	Prep	A♭7 (p. 132), F7, B♭7, E♭7	Transpose this sequence to the key of A♭ (cover up the chord column to test yourself if you want) and check against the chord finder on p. 115. Use shape 1 barre chords for A♭7 and B♭7, and shape 4 barre chords for F7 and E♭7.
2 mins	61.4 (p. 76–77)	A♭7, F7, B♭7, E♭7	Work through the sequence, thinking of the chords by their Nashville numbering steps in the key of A♭ (i.e. I7, VI7, II7 and V7). This should now be starting to make sense if you've applied the theory to both workouts at this level.

CHORD MASTER △ Pro 1

TIME	EXERCISE	CHORDS & SCALES	NOTES
2 mins	62.8 (p. 82–83)	Chords: Dm7, Am7, G7, C△, F△, B∅, E7, A7 (p. 142–149)	Use moveable chord forms throughout, using p. 142–149 of the chord library to review as necessary. Play the sequence using a quarter-note strum pattern at a moderate tempo (100–130bpm).
2 mins	Prep	Fm7, B♭7, E♭△, A♭△, D∅, G7, Cm7, C7 (p. 142–149)	Transpose this sequence to the key of Fm using the chord finder on p. 115 to verify your choices. Cover up the chord column on the left to avoid any cheating!
2 mins	62.8 (p. 82–83)	Fm7, B♭7, E♭△, A♭△, D∅, G7, Cm7, C7	Play through the sequence following the Nashville numbering symbols above the stave. **Tip:** You can also play this sequence using the eighth-note rhythm patterns on p. 20–23.
2 mins	Prep	B♭m7, E♭7, A♭△, D♭△, G∅, C7, Fm7, F7 (p. 142–149)	Transpose this sequence to the key of B♭m using the chord finder on p. 115 if necessary.
2 mins	62.8 (p. 82–83)	B♭m7, E♭7, A♭△, D♭△, G∅, C7, Fm7	Follow the Nashville numbering symbols above the stave and play the sequence. This famous sequence has been used in many tunes, from jazz standards to rock ballads – learn it in all keys for maximum fluency.

CHORD MASTER △ Pro 2

TIME	EXERCISE	CHORDS & SCALES	NOTES
2 mins	61.8 (p. 78–79)	Chords: C△, A7, Dm7, G7, E∅ (p. 142–149)	Play this sequence using a quarter-note strum pattern at a bright tempo (150–200bpm). Use moveable chord forms throughout, using pages 142–149 of the chord library to review as necessary.
2 mins	Prep	F△, D7, Gm7, C7, A∅ (p. 142–149)	Transpose this sequence to the key of F using the chord finder on p. 115 to check if needed. You can cover up the chord column on the left to give yourself an extra challenge.
2 mins	61.8 (p. 78–79)	F△, D7, Gm7, C7, A∅	Play the sequence following the Nashville numbering symbols above the stave. Use a quarter-note strum pattern, accenting beats 2 and 4 to create an authentic jazzy accompaniment.
2 mins	Prep	B♭△, G7, Cm7, F7, D∅ (p. 142–149)	Transpose this sequence to the key of B♭ using the chord finder on p. 115 to verify your choices as necessary. **Tip:** Avoid the voicings you used to play the sequence in its original key (C).
2 mins	61.8 (p. 78–79)	B♭△, G7, Cm7, F7, D∅	Play the sequence using a 'four-in-the-bar' jazz comp as before. This is the 'A' section of 'I Got Rhythm' by George Gershwin, often referred to as Rhythm Changes. Jazz musicians practise improvising over this in all keys.

Scale Master

TIME	EXERCISE	CHORDS & SCALES	NOTES
2 mins	Prep	Scale: A minor pentatonic shapes 1–5 (p. 152–153)	Review all five shapes of this scale. Skip the patterns you already know and focus on the ones you don't to maximise learning time.
2 mins	35 (p. 50)	A minor pentatonic shapes 1 and 2	Play the exercise as written, then apply the ascending/descending sequence to shape 2 of the A minor pentatonic. **Tip:** You can also play this exercise as eighth notes by setting your metronome to play without accents (i.e. on the first beat) at around 100–120bpm.
2 mins	35 (p. 50)	A minor pentatonic shape 3	Practise shape 3 of the A minor pentatonic using the same ascending/descending sequence. Remember you can also play this exercise in eighth notes if you're finding 16th notes tricky (see above).
2 mins	35 (p. 50)	A minor pentatonic shape 4	Practise shape 4 of the scale using the ascending/descending sequence. Remember to use alternate picking throughout.
2 mins	35 (p. 50)	A minor pentatonic shape 5	Apply the ascending/descending sequence to shape 5. Now that you can play all five shapes of the A minor pentatonic, apply the same approach in the primary guitar keys (E, D, G, C and F).

TIME	EXERCISE	CHORDS & SCALES	NOTES
2 mins	Prep	Scale: C major shapes 1–5 (p. 176–177)	Revise the five shapes of this scale, skimming over the ones you already know and focusing on the ones you don't to make the most of the time.
2 mins	36 (p. 51)	C major shapes 1 and 2	Complete Exercise 36 as written, then apply its ascending/descending sequence to shape 2. To play this as eighth notes, set your metronome to play without accents (i.e. on the first beat) at 100–120bpm.
2 mins	36 (p. 51)	C major shape 3	Practise shape 3 of C major using the same ascending/descending sequence. Remember to practise this exercise as eighth notes, setting your metronome at around 100–120bpm.
2 mins	36 (p. 51)	C major shape 4	Use the same ascending/descending sequence to practise shape 4 of the C major scale. Maximise your picking technique by using alternate picking throughout.
2 mins	36 (p. 51)	C major shape 5	To finish, apply the ascending/descending sequence to shape 5. Now that you can play all five shapes of the C major scale, practise them in as many different keys as you can over the next few weeks.

SCALE MASTER ▷ Intermediate 1

TIME	EXERCISE	CHORDS & SCALES	NOTES
2 mins	50 (p. 65)	Scale: A minor pentatonic shape 1 (p. 152)	Play Exercise 50 using the 'four-in-a-line' scale pattern, ascending and descending. You can easily extend this exercise across all six strings by continuing the pattern until you reach high C on the eighth fret.
2 mins	50 (p. 65)	A minor pentatonic shape 2 (p. 152)	Practise the same scale pattern again, but this time starting on the eighth fret of the sixth string, i.e. shape 2. Keep the 'four-in-a-line' sequencing as you ascend and descend.
2 mins	50 (p. 65)	A minor pentatonic shape 3 (p. 153)	Start on the tenth fret of the sixth string for shape 3 of the scale. Remember to use alternate 16th-note picking throughout and always start slowly, only setting your metronome to around 60–70bpm.
2 mins	50 (p. 65)	A minor pentatonic shape 4 (p. 153)	Shape 4 of the A minor pentatonic starts on the twelfth fret. **Tip:** Always start on the lowest note of the scale (i.e. on the sixth string), not the root note.
2 mins	50 (p. 65)	A minor pentatonic shape 5 (p. 153)	Practise shape 5 using the same ascending/descending sequence and beginning on the fifteenth fret of the sixth string. Apply the same picking pattern across all six strings of each shape. You should then transpose this workout to as many different keys as you can.

SCALE MASTER ▷ Intermediate 2

TIME	EXERCISE	CHORDS & SCALES	NOTES
2 mins	51 and 52 (p. 66–67)	Scale: C major shape 1 (p. 176)	Practise the exercises as shown using the '1-3-2-1' scale pattern ascending and descending. You can easily extend this sequence across all six strings to max up your workout.
2 mins	51 and 52 (p. 66–67)	C major shape 2 (p. 176)	Because there are now three notes on the sixth string (starting on the tenth fret), be aware that the pattern will vary slightly on some strings. Just ensure that you apply the 'up a third then descend' principle to preserve the '1-3-2-1' pattern.
2 mins	51 and 52 (p. 66–67)	C major shape 3 (p. 177)	Shape 3 of the C major scale begins on the twelfth fret of the sixth string. Always use strict alternate picking, taking care not to disrupt the down-up-down-up picking pattern.
2 mins	51 and 52 (p. 66–67)	C major shape 4 (p. 177)	We're getting quite high on the neck at this point, so begin shape 4 of the scale on the third fret, exactly as illustrated in the scale library. **Tip:** Always start on the lowest note of the scale (i.e. on the sixth string), not the root note.
2 mins	51 and 52 (p. 66–67)	C major shape 5 (p. 177)	To complete the workout, practise shape 5 using '1-3-2-1' sequencing throughout. This shape should start on the fifth fret of the sixth string. Apply the same picking pattern to the full pattern (i.e. all six strings) of each shape, then apply this workout in as many keys as you can.

TIME	EXERCISE	CHORDS & SCALES	NOTES
2 mins	55 (p. 70)	Scale: G Mixolydian mode shape 1 (p. 177)	By using the mode finder on p. 151, you will see that shape 4 of C major can be used for shape 1 of G Mixolydian. Apply the 'thirds' sequencing pattern ascending and descending. Remember that the root notes change when using the major scale as a modal-shape generator.
2 mins	55 (p. 70)	G Mixolydian mode shape 2 (p. 177)	Practise the same sequencing pattern, this time starting on the fifth fret of the sixth string. This pattern is the same as shape 5 of C major but the root notes have changed.
2 mins	55 (p. 70)	G Mixolydian mode shape 3 (p. 176)	Use shape 1 of C major to generate this shape. Use alternate 16th-note picking and start with a moderate tempo, around 80–100bpm. You can practise 'thirds' sequencing as eighth notes if you find 16ths tricky at first.
2 mins	55 (p. 70)	G Mixolydian mode shape 4 (p. 176)	Shape 4 of G Mixolydian is exactly the same as shape 2 of C major, so your first note should begin on the tenth fret. **Tip:** Always start on the lowest note of the scale (i.e. on the sixth string), not the root note (G).
2 mins	55 (p. 70)	G Mixolydian mode shape 5 (p. 177)	To practise shape 5 of G Mixolydian, start on the lowest note of shape 3 of C major. This pattern should be practised in open position and starting at the twelfth fret. The Mixolydian mode can be used to improvise over any dominant chord with major extensions (i.e. G7, G9, G11, G13, etc).

TIME	EXERCISE	CHORDS & SCALES	NOTES
2 mins	56 (p. 71)	Scale: G Phrygian dominant mode shape 1 (p. 207)	Shape 4 of C harmonic minor can be used for shape 1 of G Phrygian dominant (see mode finder on p. 151). Apply the 'sixths' sequencing pattern ascending and descending. Start slowly as this is quite a tricky exercise; if you find 16th notes too quick, use eighth notes instead at the same tempo.
2 mins	56 (p. 71)	G Phrygian dominant mode shape 2 (p. 207)	Practise the 'sixths' sequencing pattern, starting on the fourth fret of the sixth string. This pattern is the same as shape 5 of C harmonic minor but with the root note changed to G. Be aware of the new root notes when you're practising.
2 mins	56 (p. 71)	G Phrygian dominant mode shape 3 (p. 206)	Use shape 1 of C harmonic minor to generate shape 3, starting on the lowest note (7th fret). Remember to use alternate 16th-note picking throughout and always start with a moderate metronome setting of 80–100bpm.
2 mins	56 (p. 71)	G Phrygian dominant mode shape 4 (p. 206)	Phrygian dominant shape 4 is the same as C harmonic minor shape 2, so your first note begins on the tenth fret. **Tip:** Start on the lowest available note of the scale (i.e. on the sixth string), not on the root note (G).
2 mins	56 (p. 71)	G Phrygian dominant mode shape 5 (p. 207)	Practise shape 5 of this mode starting on the thirteenth fret and in open position to ensure maximum fingerboard coverage. This shape is generated using shape 3 of C harmonic minor. Use the Phrygian dominant mode to improvise over any dominant chord with minor extensions (i.e. G7+, G7♭9, G7♯9, G7♭9sus, etc).

Damping and Muting

TIME	EXERCISE	CHORDS & SCALES	NOTES
1 min	Prep	Chords: C (p. 116), Am (p. 134)	Review both chord shapes. Warm up your picking technique using your thumb (*p*) to play the fifth string, while simultaneously picking the fourth, third and second strings with *i*, *m* and *a*.
2 mins	15 (p. 30)	C, Am	Play through this exercise starting slowly at around 70bpm. **Tip**: Start by playing the bass notes only, gradually introducing the chords, beginning with C on beat 1.
2 mins	15 (p. 30)	C, Am	Position your picking-hand palm so that it's just touching the fifth and sixth strings, close to the bridge. Play Exercise 15 several times. You'll need to experiment with your picking-hand position to find the 'sweet spot' where the bass notes are just slightly damped.
1 min	Prep	F (p. 126), G (open – p. 130, barre – p. 131)	Review both shapes. The F should be played as a full barre chord (a good fretting-hand stamina builder!), while the G can be fretted open or as a full barre chord on the third fret.
4 mins	61.2 (p. 76–77)	C, Am, F, G	Play through the sequence, using the palm-muting technique described above. Remember to switch the bass pattern on the F and G chords, starting with the root on the sixth string.

TIME	EXERCISE	CHORDS & SCALES	NOTES
1 min	Prep	Chords: G5, C5 (p. 141)	If you don't know these power-chord shapes already, get to know them. You can find them in the chord library on p. 141.
2 mins	3 (p. 18)	G5, C5	Instead of playing the chords used in this exercise, you need to substitute G5 (for E) and C5 (for Am). Play them with down-strums as indicated, but keep your pick sweep shallow to ensure that only the fifth and sixth strings are sounded.
2 mins	3 (p. 18)	C (p. 116), Am (p. 134)	Position your picking-hand palm close to the bridge, so that it touches just the fifth and sixth strings, and play the exercise several times. Try altering your hand position to achieve varying degrees of muting.
1 min	Prep	A5 (p. 140), F5 (p. 141)	You can use the sixth-string power-chord shape (G5) for both chords. To play A5, move the shape up two frets; to play F5 move it down two frets.
4 mins	61.2 (p. 76–77)	C5, A5, F5, G5	Instead of playing the major and minor chords indicated, you can substitute power chords throughout, using the shapes prepped above. Use palm-muting throughout. **Tip**: Try playing eighth-note down-strums for a heavier sound.

TIME	EXERCISE	CHORDS & SCALES	NOTES
1 min	Prep	Chords: C (p. 116), Am (p. 134)	Review the chords if necessary. Warm up your picking technique using your thumb (*p*) and fingers (*i*, *m* and *a*) to pick the strings individually (i.e. no pinches). **Tip:** Alternate your string picking order to gain greater finger independence.
2 mins	19 (p. 34)	C, Am	Play through this exercise starting slowly, at around 70bpm. Begin with the bassline (thumb only) and gradually introduce the melody notes one at a time. This is the quickest way to learn any picking pattern.
2 mins	19 (p. 34)	C, Am	Position your picking-hand palm so that it's just resting on the bottom three strings close to the bridge. Play the exercise several times. Experiment with your hand position to find the 'sweet spot' where the bass notes are damped but the pitch is still audible.
1 min	Prep	F (p. 126), G (p. 130)	Review these shapes. The F can be played using your thumb to fret the sixth string, with your remaining fingers on the higher strings (omit the first and fifth strings). The G can be played open using only your third finger to fret the bass note.
4 mins	61.2 (p. 76–77)	C, Am, F, G	Play this sequence using the palm-muting technique described above. Switch the bass pattern on the F and G chords, starting with the root on the sixth string (keep the second bass note on the fourth string).

TIME	EXERCISE	CHORDS & SCALES	NOTES
1 min	Prep	Chords: D5 (p. 140), C5, G5 (p. 141)	Revise these chords if necessary. Practise moving quickly between the shapes, keeping your fingers in contact with the strings at all times.
2 mins	10 (p. 25)	D5, C5, G5	Play the exercise exactly as written – don't add any palm muting with your picking hand yet. Concentrate on achieving slick chord changes with no gaps. Keep to a moderate tempo, between 80–100bpm.
2 mins	10 (p. 25)	D5, C5, G5	Now position your palm close to the bridge so that it just touches the fourth and fifth strings. Run through the exercise several times. Keep your pick attack light and consistent: too much force will cause your pick to dig into the strings, creating an erratic delivery.
1 min	Prep	A5 (p. 140), F5 (p. 141), G5	You can use the sixth-string power-chord shape (i.e. G5) for all three chords. Practise moving quickly along the neck by releasing the pressure of your fretting fingers and sliding them along the strings.
4 mins	62.4 (p. 80–81)	A5, F5, G5	Use power chords to play this example. Repeat the rhythm given in the first bar of Exercise 10 throughout. This famous sequence can be heard in many tunes, including 'All Along the Watchtower' and 'Stairway to Heaven'. Play it in as many keys as you can!

TIME	EXERCISE	CHORDS & SCALES	NOTES
1 min	Prep	Chords: Am (p. 135), Dm (p. 121)	Use the barre chords indicated in the chord library for both shapes. Ensure that you can change quickly and efficiently between both chords on the fifth fret.
2 mins	9 (p. 24)	Am, Dm	Start slowly and play this exercise at around 60bpm. Sound the top three strings of each chord by focusing your pick on the higher strings; mute the chord by releasing the pressure of your fretting hand (don't use your picking hand to mute the strings).
2 mins	9 (p. 24)	Am, Dm	Play Exercise 9 again, but this time fret the chords with minimal finger pressure to create a percussive, Bob Marley-style 'skank'. **Tip**: Play swing (shuffle) 16ths for an old-school reggae vibe.
1 min	Prep	F△ (p. 142), G7 (p. 131), C△ (p. 142), E7 (p. 125)	Select the fifth-string-root moveable shape for F△ and C△ from the pages indicated in the chord library. Use your first finger to barre across the strings, ensuring that the first string is fretted.
4 mins	61.6 (p. 78–79)	F△, G7, C△, E7	Play through the sequence using the fretting-hand muting technique described above. Aim your pick onto the top strings only, fretting each chord lightly to keep the sound percussive and tight.

TIME	EXERCISE	CHORDS & SCALES	NOTES
1 min	12 (p. 27)	Chords: Am7 (p. 27), D9 (p. 146–147)	Practise forming the Am7 chord as shown in this exercise, using your third finger to form a semi-barre across the higher strings. You'll find this shape invaluable for changing quickly to ninth chords on the same fret.
2 mins	12 (p. 27)	Am7, D9	Play the exercise starting slowly at the lowest tempo (55bpm) to ensure that your rhythm is accurate. Don't worry about playing the rests at this stage. **Tip**: Maintain a strict 16th-note strumming pattern throughout for optimum rhythmic accuracy.
2 mins	12 (p. 27)	Am7, D9	Now play the exercise again but, this time, focus on keeping all of your chords short and percussive (except the tie onto the third beat in each bar). Achieve this by releasing the pressure of your fretting hand immediately after playing the chord.
1 min	Prep	Gm7, C9, F△, Bø, E7#9 (p. 142–149)	Practise changing quickly between all these shapes. To play Gm7 and C9, simply move the Am7 and D9 shapes two frets lower. F△ should be played as a fifth-string-root chord on the eighth fret. Play both Bø and E7#9 on the sixth fret.
4 mins	62.6 (p. 82–83)	Am7, Gm7, C9, F△, Bø, E7#9	To finish, work through this sequence using the fretting-hand muting technique described above. This famous sequence has featured in many tunes, including 'Sunny'. Practise it in as many different keys as possible.

Technique Buster

TIME	EXERCISE	CHORDS & SCALES	NOTES
1 min	25 (p. 40)		Practise this exercise at the slowest suggested tempo (70bpm). Focus on keeping your alternate picking even and consistent. Keep your pick at 90° to the strings to ensure your picking is always consistent.
1 min	25 (p. 40)		This time, move the pattern across to the fifth string, starting on the fifth fret with your first finger. **Tip:** Use all four fretting-hand fingers (one per fret) to max up your technique busting.
2 mins	25 (p. 40)		Now play the pattern on the fourth and then third strings. Keep your starting note (using your first finger) on the fifth fret as before.
2 mins	25 (p. 40)		Play the pattern on the third and then second strings – keep your starting note (using your first finger) on the fifth fret. Always practise with a metronome to keep the sequence even and consistent, pausing between string changes only.
4 mins	25 (p. 40)		To round off this workout, play the sequence starting on the sixth string and ascend to the first without pausing (playing the sequence once on each string only), then descend in the same way. You can now use this exercise as a great warm-up, starting on any fret.

TIME	EXERCISE	CHORDS & SCALES	NOTES
2 mins	Prep	Scale: A minor pentatonic shapes 1–5 (p. 152–153)	Review all five shapes of this scale. **Tip:** Skip the patterns you already know and focus on the ones you don't to maximise your learning time.
2 mins	53 (p. 68)	A minor pentatonic shapes 1 and 2	Play the exercise as written then apply the same sequencing pattern to shape 2 of the A minor pentatonic. Use the finger-rolling technique described in the exercise when playing notes on adjacent strings.
2 mins	53 (p. 68)	A minor pentatonic shape 3	Practise shape 3 of the A minor pentatonic scale using the same sequencing pattern as before. Remember that you only play one note on the third string before descending. Use alternate picking throughout for maximum technique busting!
2 mins	53 (p. 68)	A minor pentatonic shape 4	Apply the sequencing pattern to A minor pentatonic shape 4, starting on the twelfth fret. **Tip:** You can also practise this shape in open position.
2 mins	53 (p. 68)	A minor pentatonic shape 5	Practise shape 5 of the A minor pentatonic starting on the third fret (as illustrated in the scale library). Now that you can play all five shapes of the A minor pentatonic, practise in the primary keys of Em, Dm and Gm.

TECHNIQUE BUSTER △ Intermediate 1

TIME	EXERCISE	CHORDS & SCALES	NOTES
1 min	33 (p. 48)		When you first play this exercise, begin at the lowest tempo (60 bpm). Listen carefully to the notes you're producing: do the up-picks sound different from the down-picks? With practice, both pick strokes should sound identical.
1 min	33 (p. 48)		Now move the pattern to the fifth string, starting with your first finger on the fifth fret. **Tip:** Use all four fretting-hand fingers (one per fret) to maximise your technique busting.
2 mins	33 (p. 48)		Spend some time playing the pattern on the fourth and then third strings. Keep your starting note (using your first finger) on the fifth fret as before.
2 mins	33 (p. 48)		Keeping your starting note (using your first finger) on the fifth fret as before, play the pattern on the third and then second strings. Keep your pick at 90° to the strings and try to minimise your picking action, which should be a combination of fingers and wrist movement.
4 mins	33 (p. 48)		Play the sequence again, starting on the sixth string, jumping to the string above after playing the last note on the sixth fret. If you wish, pause before descending in the same way. **Tip:** This workout can be played as a warm-up, starting on any fret of the sixth string.

TECHNIQUE BUSTER △ Intermediate 2

TIME	EXERCISE	CHORDS & SCALES	NOTES
2 mins	Prep	Scale: A minor pentatonic shapes 1–5 (p. 152–153)	Revise all five shapes of this scale. **Tip:** To make the most of your time, skip the patterns you know well and focus on the ones you're less familiar with.
2 mins	54 (p. 69)	A minor pentatonic shapes 1 and 2	Play Exercise 54 normally, then apply its sequencing pattern to shape 2 of the A minor pentatonic. Play the second group of notes starting on the fourth string (shape 2) with your third, second and fourth fingers.
2 mins	54 (p. 69)	A minor pentatonic shape 3	Practise shape 3 of the A minor pentatonic using the same sequencing pattern as before. Remember to only play one note on the third string before descending. This exercise is impossible without using the finger-rolling technique described in the text.
2 mins	54 (p. 69)	A minor pentatonic shape 4	This time, apply the sequencing pattern to shape 4 of the A minor pentatonic scale, starting on the twelfth fret. **Tip:** You can also practise this shape in open position.
2 mins	54 (p. 69)	A minor pentatonic shape 5	Finally, practise shape 5 of the A minor pentatonic starting on the third fret (as shown in the scale library). Now that you can play all five shapes of this scale, practise it in the primary keys of Em, Dm and Gm.

TIME	EXERCISE	CHORDS & SCALES	NOTES
1 min	57 (p. 72)	Scale: C major shape 1 (p. 176)	Practise this triad exercise as written, paying particular attention to the alternate picking indicated. Don't be tempted to rush: start slowly around 60–80bpm. **Tip:** Accent the first note of each triplet group for a more advanced workout.
2 mins	57 (p. 72)	C major shape 1	Extend the sequence beginning with a C triad, starting on the fourth string, tenth fret. Keep within the parameters of shape 1 of the scale. Your final triad should be an F major starting on the third string, fret 10.
2 mins	58 (p. 73)	C major shape 1	This pattern descends from the C triad you started on, above. Keep your fingers close to the strings at all times, as this will minimise muscle movement and ultimately enable you to play faster.
2 mins	58 (p. 73)	C major shape 1	Extend this sequence by starting on the high F triad that you finished on, above. Keep within the parameters of the shape 1 scale shape. Your final triad should be the C triad that the previous pattern started on.
3 mins	57 and 58 (p. 72–73)	C major shape 1	Now you can practise playing the entire sequence of ascending and descending triads across the full shape 1 pattern of the C major scale. This invaluable technique workout should be applied to the remaining four shapes of C major, then practised in all keys!

TIME	EXERCISE	CHORDS & SCALES	NOTES
2 mins	59 (p. 74)	Scale: C major shape 1 (p. 176)	Run through this arpeggio exercise using the alternate picking indicated. Start slowly at 60bpm – don't be tempted to rush. **Tip:** Try accenting the first note of each 16th note grouping to max up your technique busting.
2 mins	60 (p. 75)	C major shape 1	Practise the descending sequence, which begins on the first string, seventh fret. Always use finger rolling when playing adjacent notes on the same fret.
2 mins	59 and 60 (p. 74–75)	C major shape 1	Combine the previous two parts of the workout to create a four-bar ascending/descending arpeggio sequence. If you prefer, you can play the ascending upper octave of C△ on the fourth beat of bar 2. Your last note (B) will need to be repeated to begin descending in bar 3.
2 mins	59 and 60 (p. 74–75)	C major shape 2 (p. 177)	Now transfer your arpeggio sequence to shape 2 of the C major scale. Your first arpeggio should be Dm7, beginning on the tenth fret. Remember to keep within the boundaries of the shape 2 scale pattern.
2 mins	59 and 60 (p. 74–75)	C major shape 3 (p. 177)	To finish your workout, transfer the arpeggio sequence to shape 3 of the C major scale, starting with Em7 on the twelfth fret. The next time you practise this workout, start at section 3. You will then be able to add the remaining scale patterns, shape 4 and shape 5.

Notation guide

Open position (first
fret) chord box:

Chord box beginning
on fifth fret:

✕ open string not played
O open string (root note) played
O open string (chord note) played
● root note
● chord note
●—● barre or semi-barre

Note: Circled numbers indicate
correct fretting-hand fingering.
Occasionally, alternate fingering
will be shown in brackets.

Chord Library

I	♭II	II	♭III	III	IV	♯IV/♭V	V	♯V/♭VI	VI	♭VII	VII
C	D♭	D	E♭	E	F	F♯/G♭	G	G♯/A♭	A	B♭	B
C♯/D♭	D	D♯/E♭	E	F	F♯/G♭	G	G♯/A♭	A	A♯/B♭	B	C
D	E♭	E	F	F♯	G	G♯/A♭	A	A♯/B♭	B	C	C♯
D♯/E♭	E	F	F♯/G♭	G	G♯/A♭	A	A♯/B♭	B	C	C♯/D♭	D
E	F	F♯	G	G♯	A	A♯/B♭	B	C	C♯	D	D♯
F	G♭	G	A♭	A	B♭	B	C	C♯/D♭	D	E♭	E
F♯/G♭	G	G♯/A♭	A	A♯/B♭	B	C	C♯/D♭	D	D♯/E♭	E	F
G	A♭	A	B♭	B	C	C♯/D♭	D	D♯/E♭	E	F	F♯
G♯/A♭	A	A♯/ B♭	B	C	C♯/D♭	D	D♯/E♭	E	F	F♯/G♭	G
A	B♭	B	C	C♯	D	D♯/E♭	E	F	F♯	G	G♯
A♯/B♭	B	C	C♯/D♭	D	D♯/E♭	E	F	F♯/G♭	G	G♯/A♭	A
B	C	C♯	D	D♯	E	F	F♯	G	G♯	A	A♯

Chord Library

C

1 C major

1 C minor

1 C7

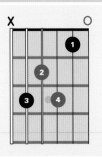

2 C major

8

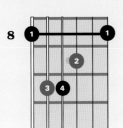

2 C minor

8

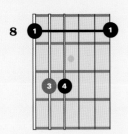

2 C7

8

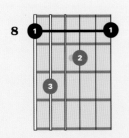

1 C#/Db major

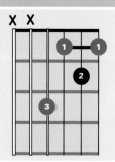

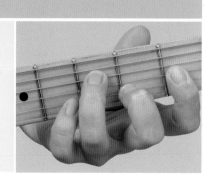

1 C#/Db minor

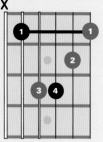

1 C#7/Db7

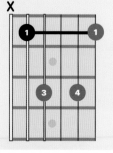

2 C#/D♭ major

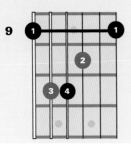

2 C#/D♭ minor

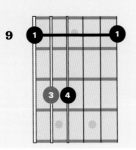

2 C#7/D♭7

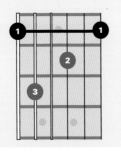

Chord Library

D

1   D major

X X O

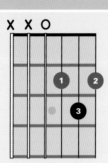

1   D minor

X X O

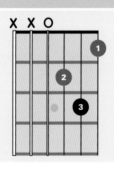

1   D7

X X O

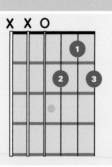

2 D major

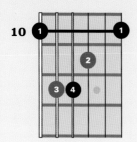

10

2 D minor

X

5

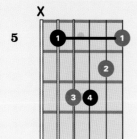

2 D7

X

5

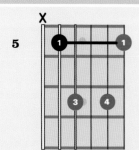

E♭/D♯

1 E♭/D♯ major

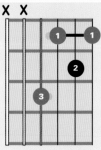

1 E♭/D♯ minor

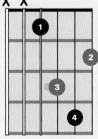

1 E♭7/D♯7

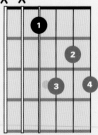

2 E♭/D♯ major

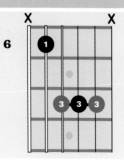

2 E♭/D♯ minor

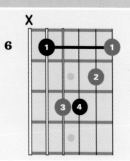

2 E♭7/D♯7

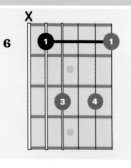

1 E major

1 E minor

1 E7

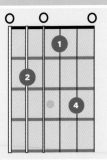

2 E major

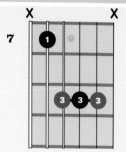 

2 E minor

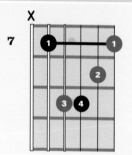 

2 E7

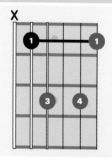 

Chord Library

F

1 F major

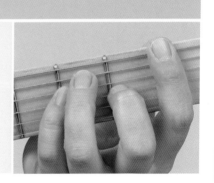

1 F minor

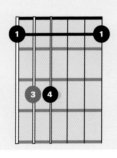

1 F7

2 F major

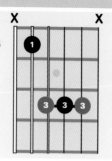
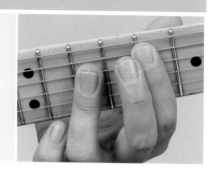

2 F minor

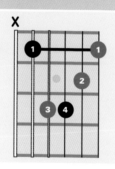

2 F7

1 F♯/G♭ major

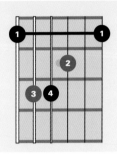

1 F♯/G♭ minor

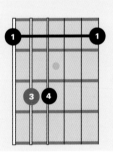

1 F♯7/G♭7

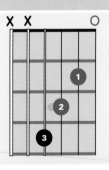

2 F#/G♭ major

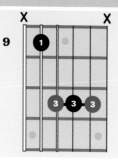

2 F#/G♭ minor

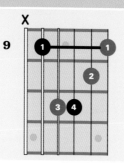

2 F#7/G♭7

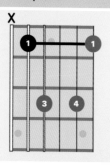

1 G major

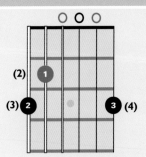

1 G minor

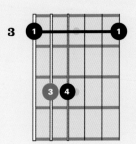

1 G7

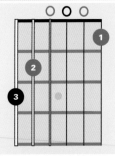

2 G major

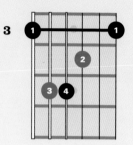

3

2 G minor

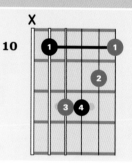

X

10

2 G7

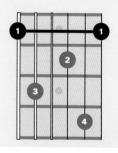

3

G♯/A♭

1 G♯/A♭ major

4

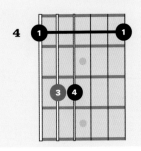 

1 G♯/A♭ minor

4

1 G♯7/A♭7

4

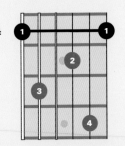 

2   G#/A♭ major

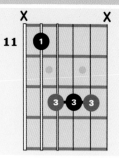

2   G#/A♭ minor

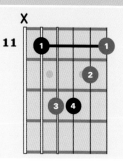

2   G#7/A♭7

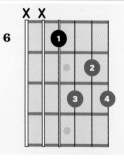

1   A major

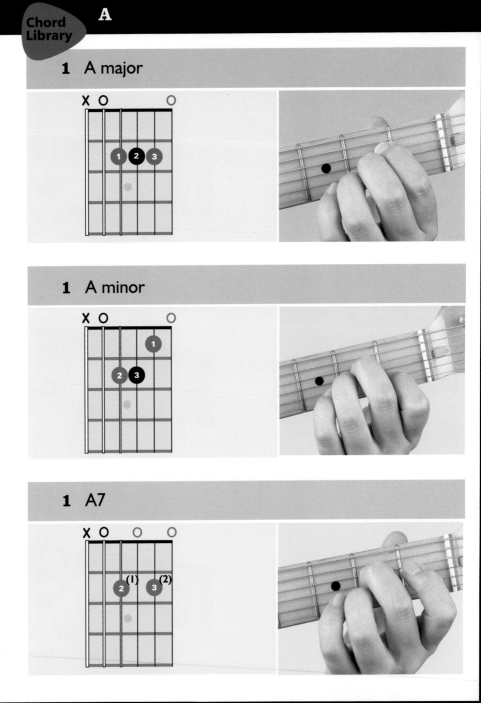

1   A minor

1   A7

2 A major

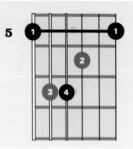

5

2 A minor

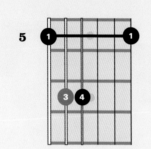

5

2 A7

5

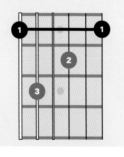

A#/B♭

1 A#/B♭ major

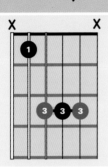

1 A#/B♭ minor

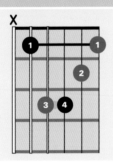

1 A#7/B♭7

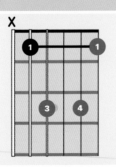

2 A♯/B♭ major

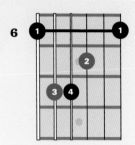

2 A♯/B♭ minor

2 A♯7/B♭7

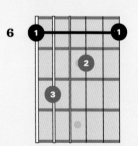

B

1 B major

1 B minor

1 B7

2 B major

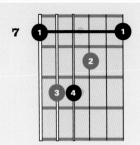

2 B minor

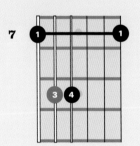

2 B7

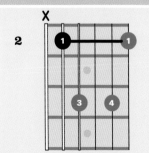

Power Chords

E5 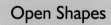 Open Shapes

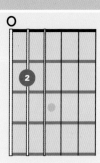

A5

D5

G5

C5

F5

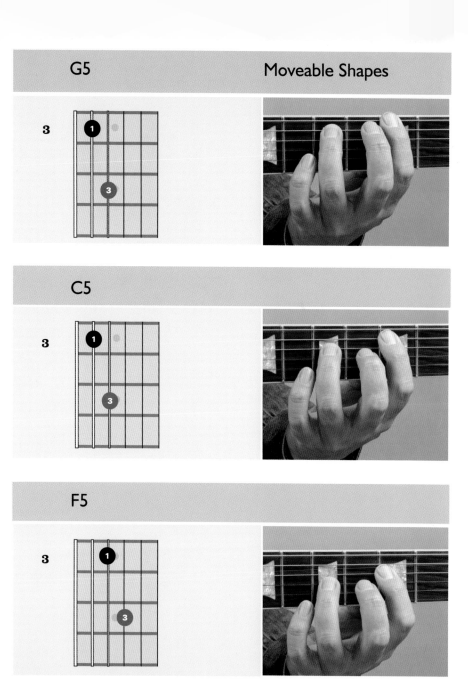

Major Seventh Chords

C△   Open Shapes

A△

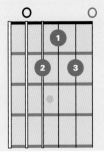

F△

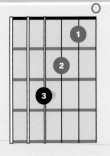

A△   Moveable Shapes

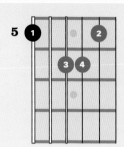

D△

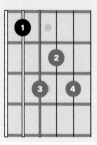

G△

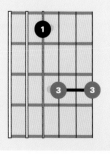

Minor Seventh Chords

Em7 — Open Shapes

Am7

Dm7

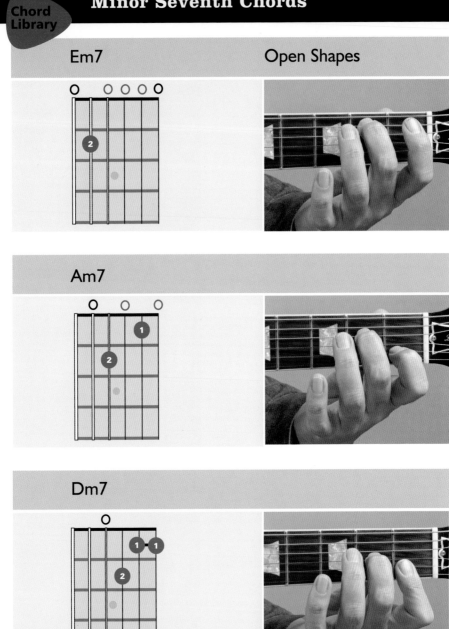

Am7

5

Moveable Shapes

Dm7

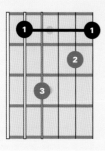

5

Gm7

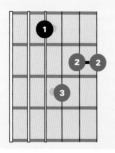

5

Chord Library

Dominant 9/11/13 Chords

E9

Moveable Shapes

6

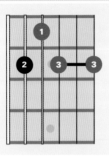

E7♯9

6

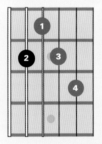

E7♭9

6

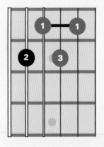

A11

Moveable Shapes

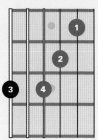

3

D11

3

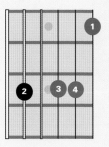

A13

5

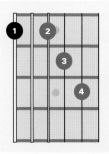

Diminished Chords

A°

Moveable Shapes

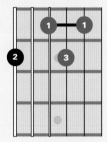

E♭°

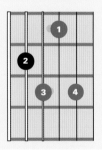

G°

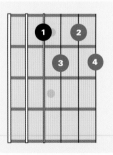

Half-Diminished Chords

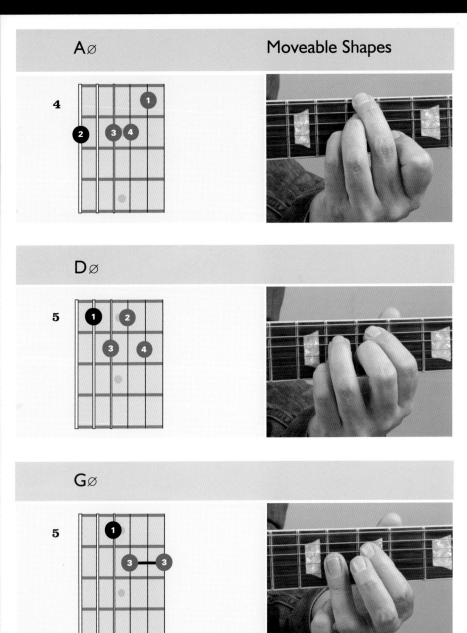

A∅

Moveable Shapes

D∅

G∅

Chapter 4

Scale Library

Use this scale to create this mode	Major shape 1	Major shape 2	Major shape 3	Major shape 4	Major shape 5	Harmonic Minor shape 4
Dorian		(lowest note becomes new root)				
Phrygian			(lowest note becomes new root)			
Lydian			(second note becomes new root)			
Mixolydian				(lowest note becomes new root)		
Aeolian					(lowest note becomes new root)	
Locrian	(lowest note becomes new root)					
Phrygian Dominant						(lowest note becomes new root)

Note: Only shape 1 of each mode is given.

Notation guide

Open position (first fret) scale box:

Scale box starting at the seventh fret:

✗	open string not played
O	open string (root note) played
O	open string (chord note) played
●	root note
●	scale note

Note: Circled numbers indicate correct fretting-hand fingering.

A Minor Pentatonic

SHAPE 1

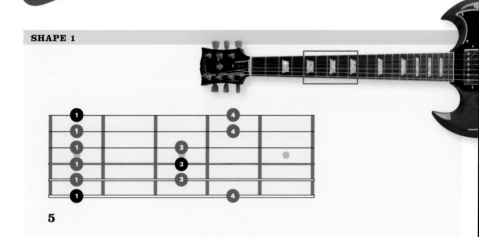

5

SHAPE 2

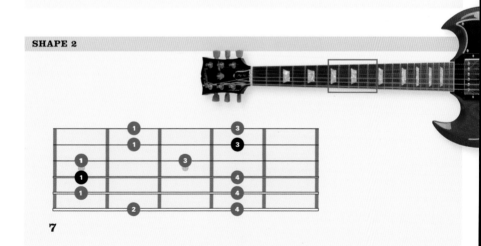

7

SHAPE 3

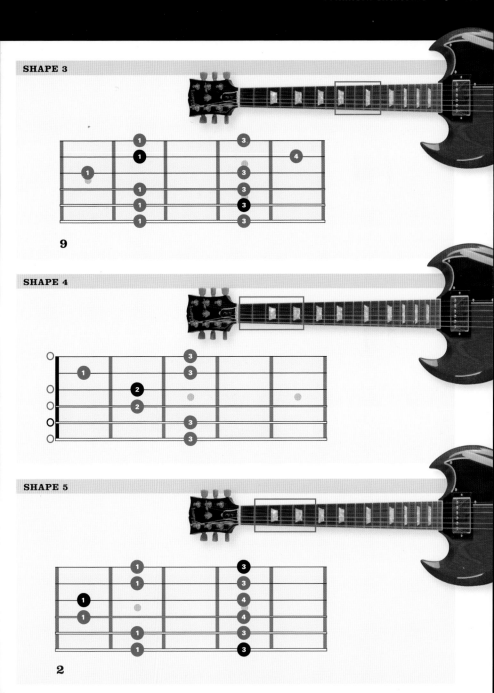

9

SHAPE 4

SHAPE 5

2

B♭ Minor Pentatonic

SHAPE 1

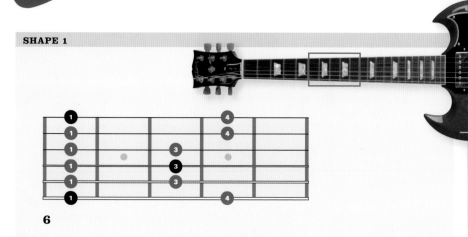

6

SHAPE 2

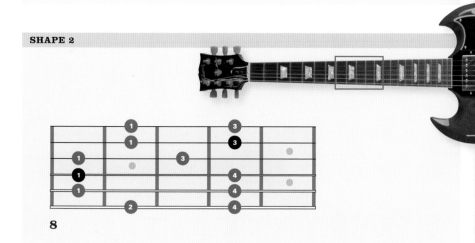

8

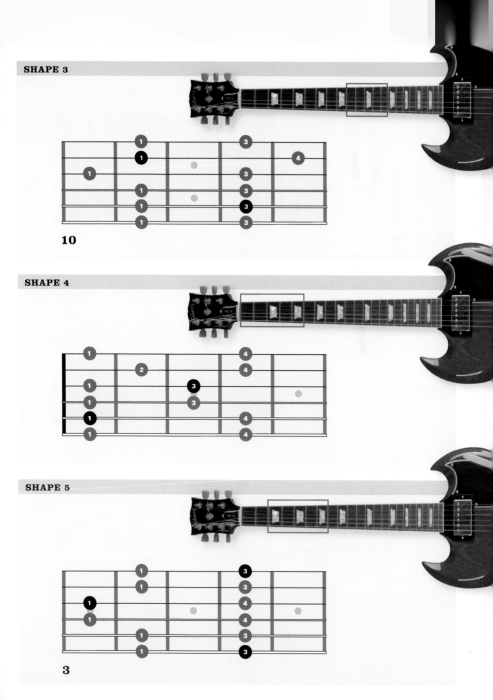

SHAPE 3

10

SHAPE 4

SHAPE 5

3

SHAPE 1

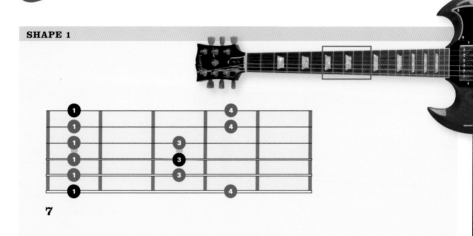

7

SHAPE 2

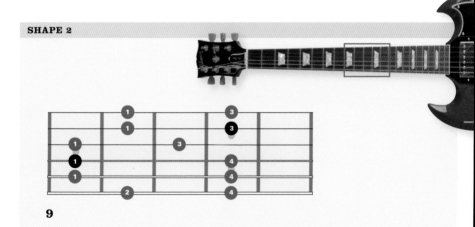

9

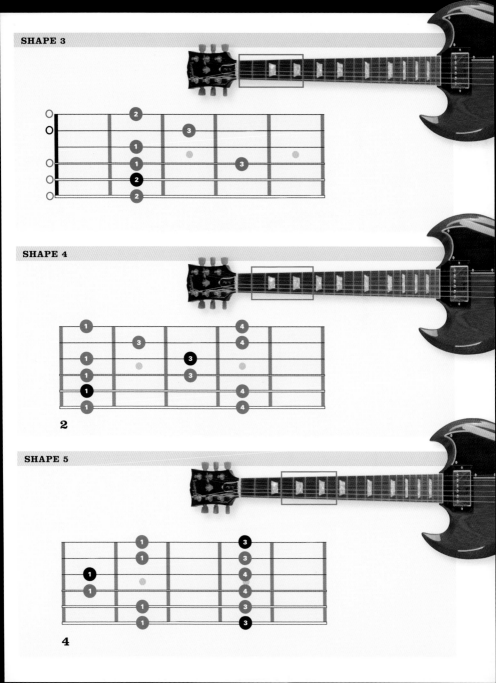

SHAPE 3

SHAPE 4

2

SHAPE 5

4

SHAPE 1

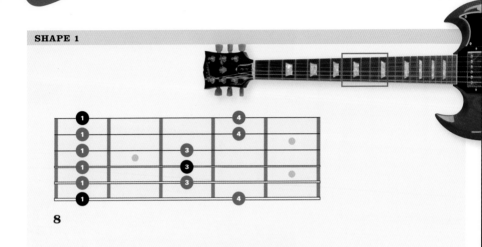

8

SHAPE 2

10

SHAPE 3

SHAPE 4

SHAPE 5

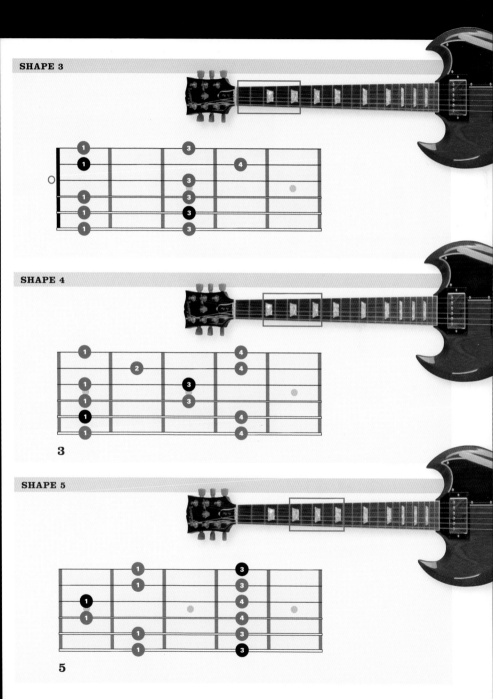

C# Minor Pentatonic

SHAPE 1

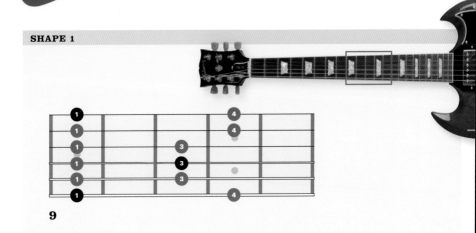

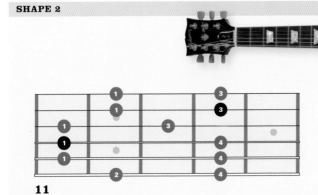

9

SHAPE 2

11

SHAPE 3

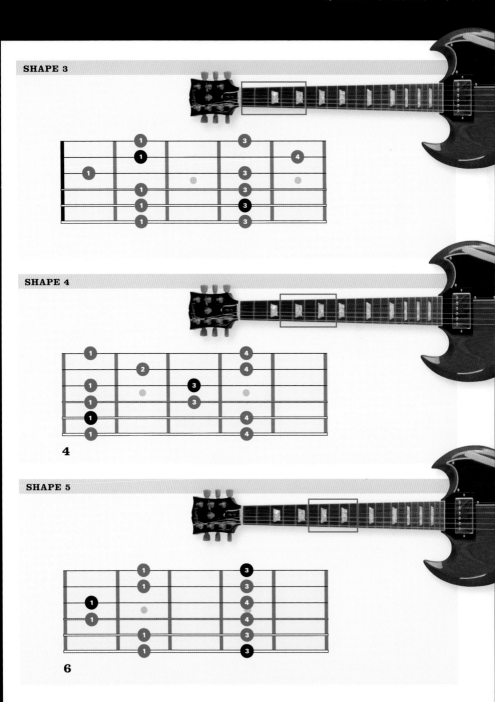

SHAPE 4

4

SHAPE 5

6

D Minor Pentatonic

SHAPE 1

10

SHAPE 2

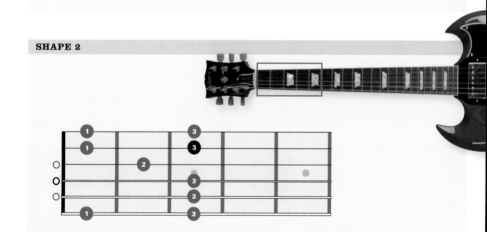

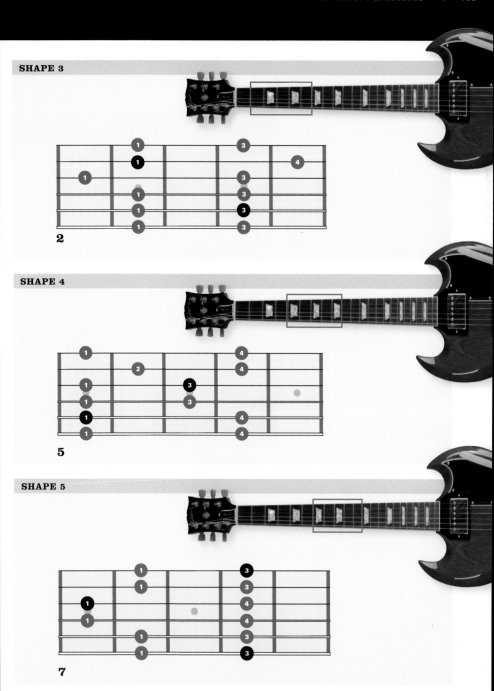

SHAPE 3

2

SHAPE 4

5

SHAPE 5

7

E♭ Minor Pentatonic

SHAPE 1

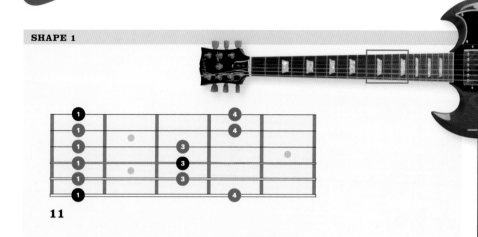

11

SHAPE 2

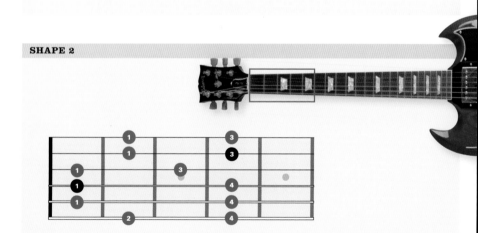

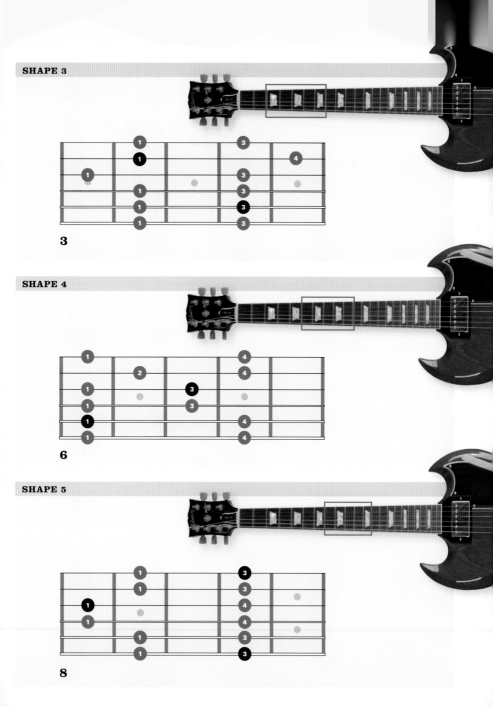

SHAPE 3

3

SHAPE 4

6

SHAPE 5

8

E Minor Pentatonic

SHAPE 1

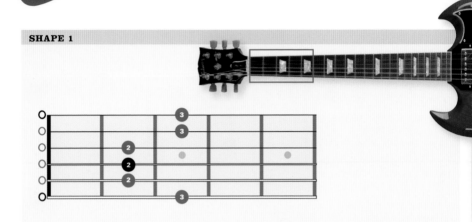

SHAPE 2

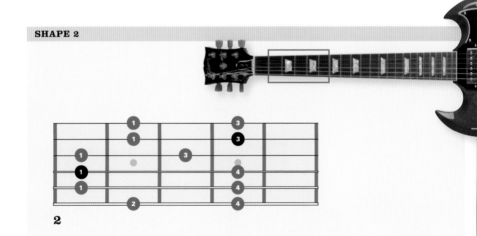

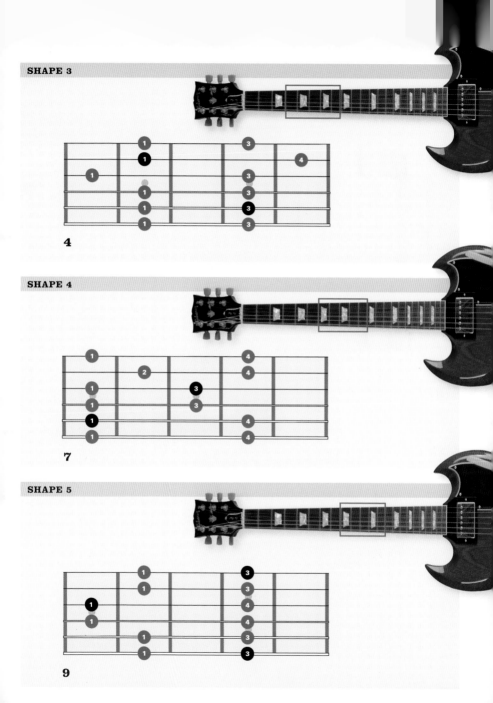

F Minor Pentatonic

SHAPE 1

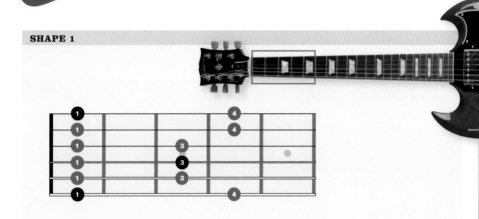

SHAPE 2

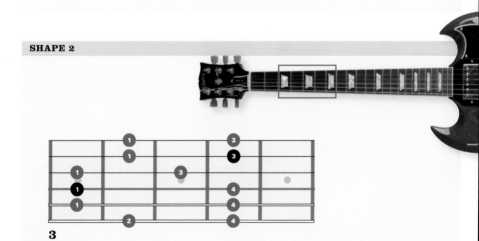

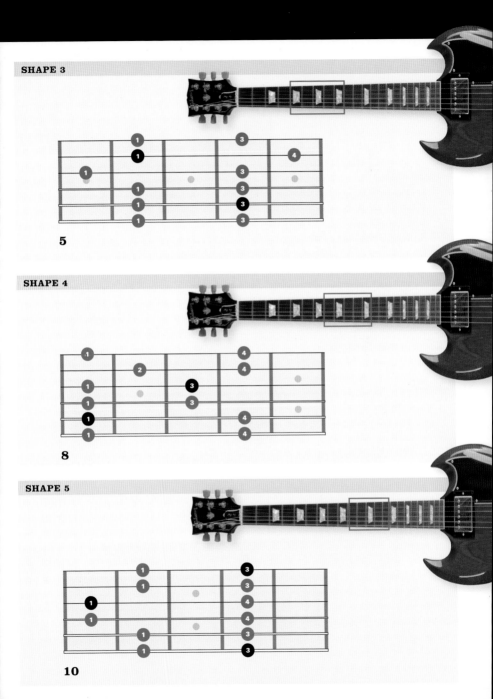

SHAPE 3

5

SHAPE 4

8

SHAPE 5

10

F# Minor Pentatonic

SHAPE 1

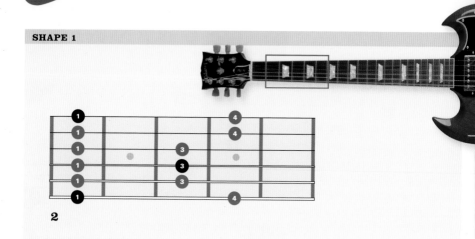

2

SHAPE 2

4

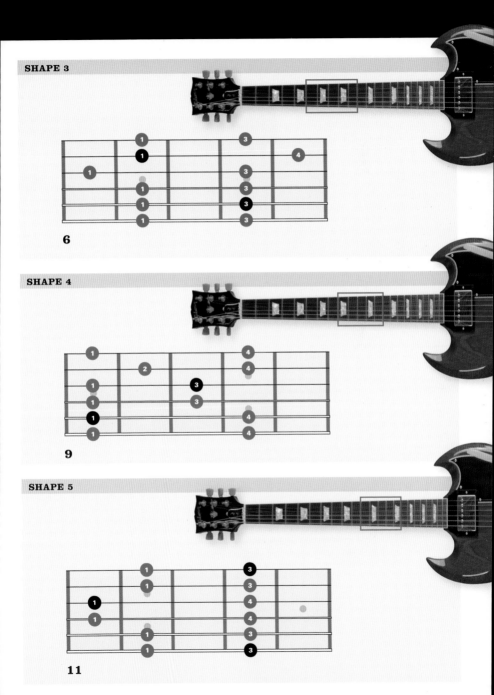

SHAPE 3

6

SHAPE 4

9

SHAPE 5

11

G Minor Pentatonic

SHAPE 1

3

SHAPE 2

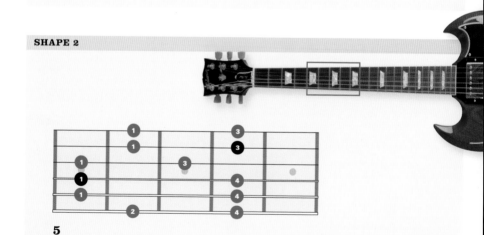

5

SHAPE 3

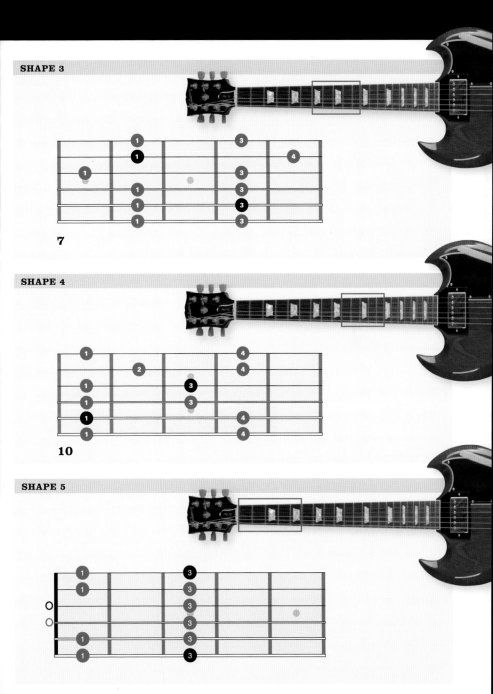

7

SHAPE 4

10

SHAPE 5

G# Minor Pentatonic

SHAPE 1

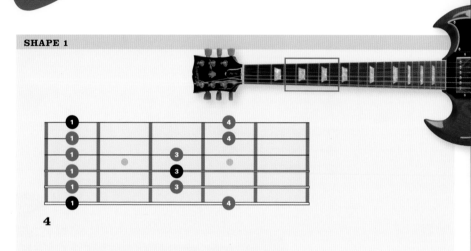

SHAPE 2

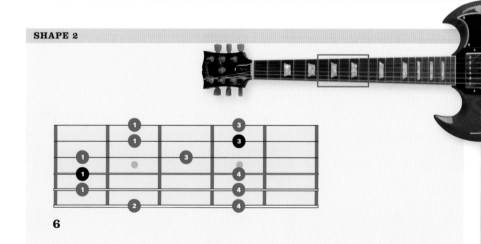

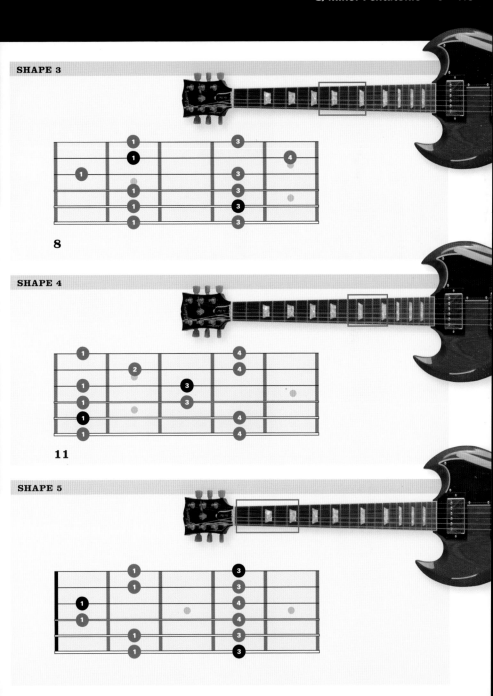

SHAPE 3

8

SHAPE 4

11

SHAPE 5

C Major

SHAPE 1

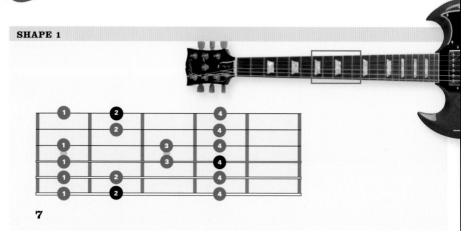

7

SHAPE 2

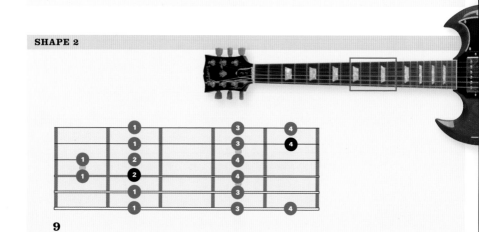

9

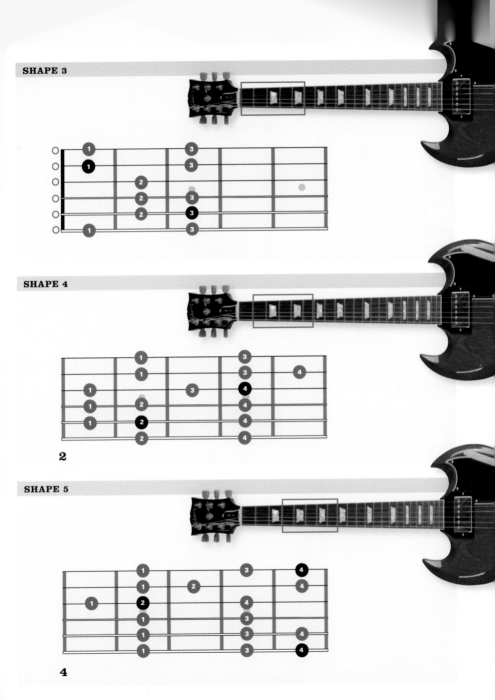

SHAPE 3

SHAPE 4

2

SHAPE 5

4

C#/D♭ Major

SHAPE 1

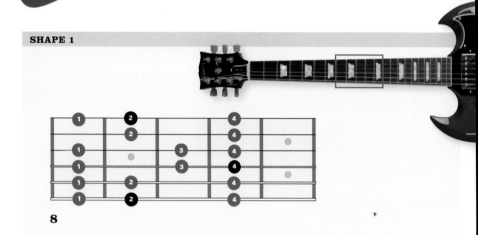

8

SHAPE 2

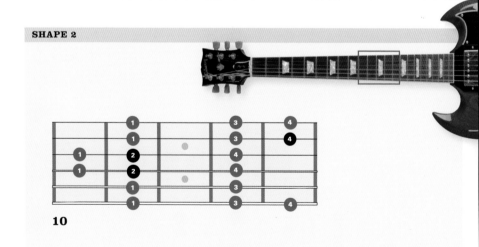

10

SHAPE 3

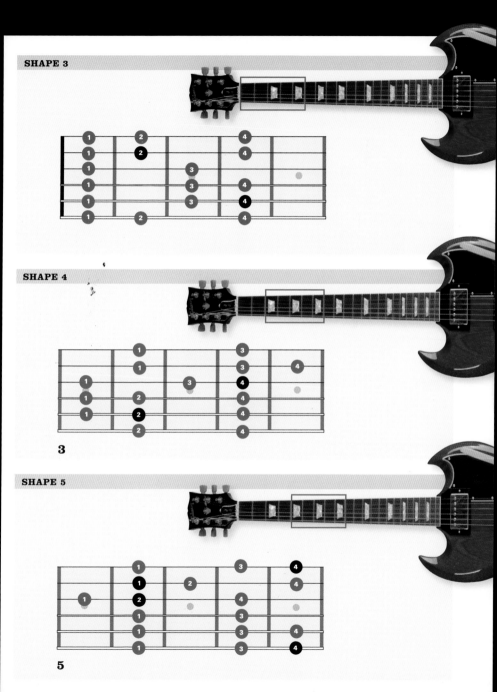

SHAPE 4

3

SHAPE 5

5

D Major

SHAPE 1

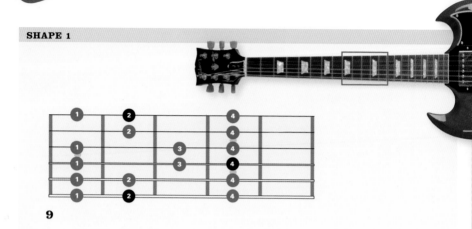

9

SHAPE 2

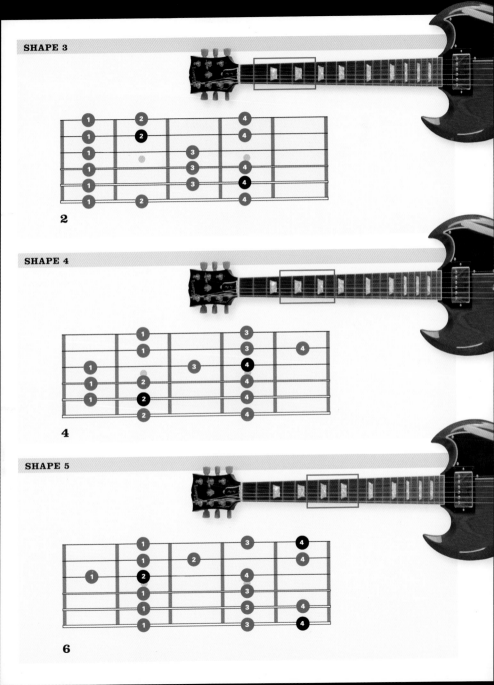

SHAPE 3

2

SHAPE 4

4

SHAPE 5

6

D#/E♭ Major

SHAPE 1

10

SHAPE 2

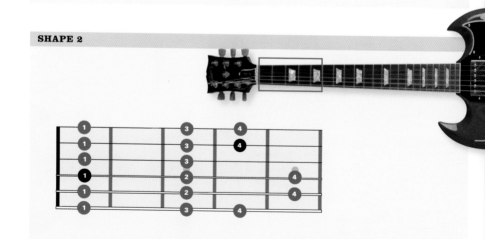

SHAPE 3

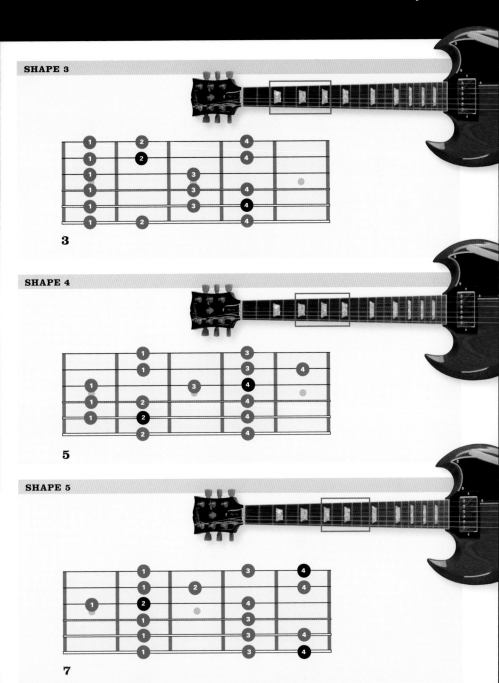

3

SHAPE 4

5

SHAPE 5

7

E Major

SHAPE 1

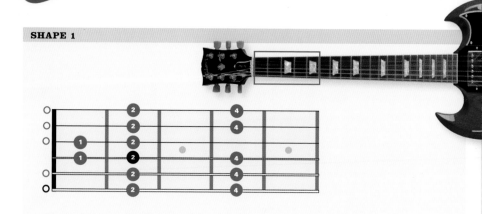

SHAPE 2

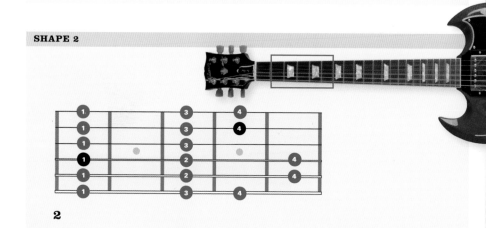

2

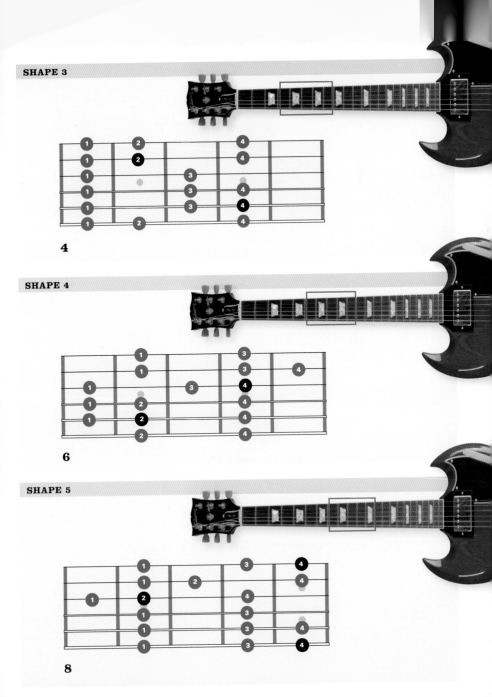

SHAPE 3

4

SHAPE 4

6

SHAPE 5

8

Scale Library

F Major

SHAPE 1

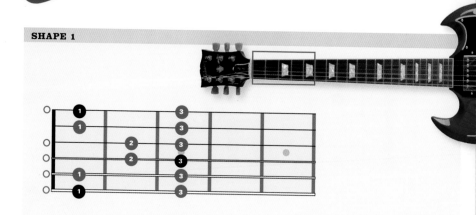

SHAPE 2

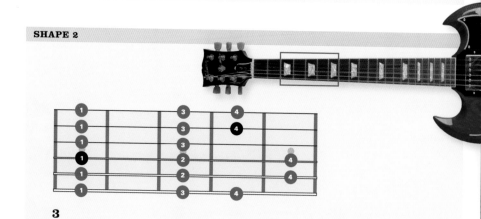

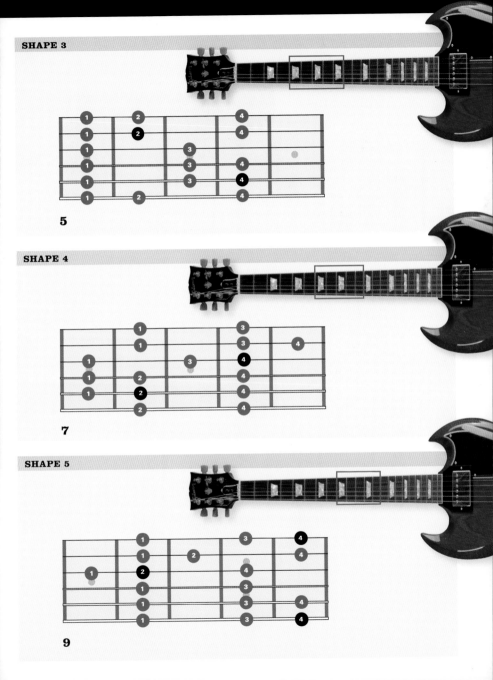

SHAPE 3

5

SHAPE 4

7

SHAPE 5

9

F♯/G♭ Major

SHAPE 1

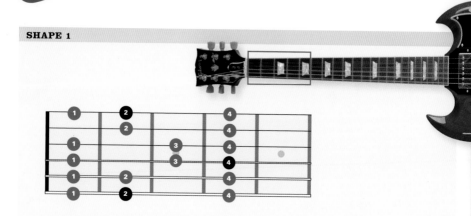

SHAPE 2

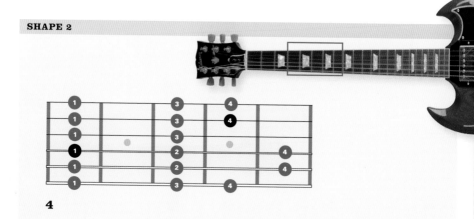

4

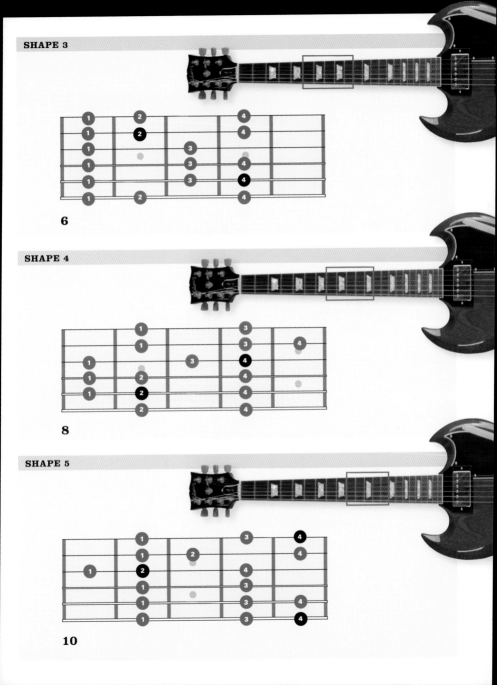

SHAPE 3

6

SHAPE 4

8

SHAPE 5

10

G Major

SHAPE 1

2

SHAPE 2

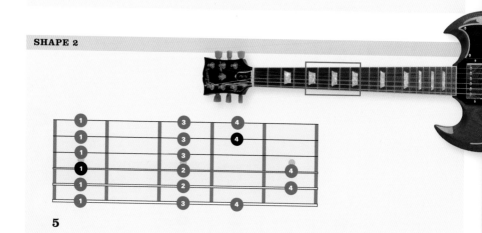

5

SHAPE 3

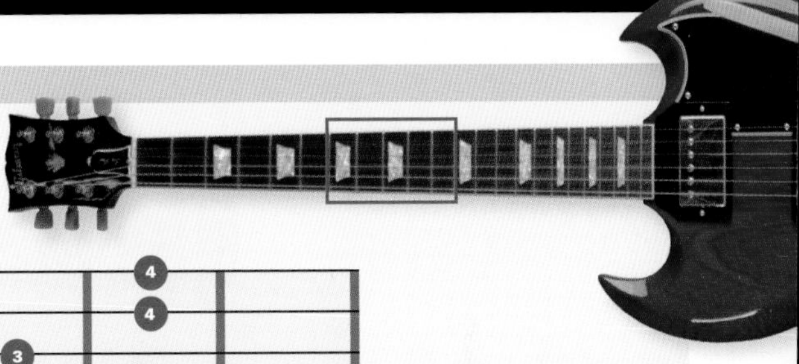

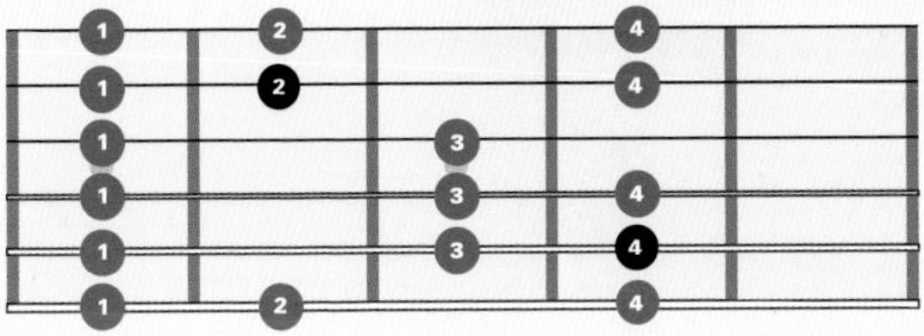

7

SHAPE 4

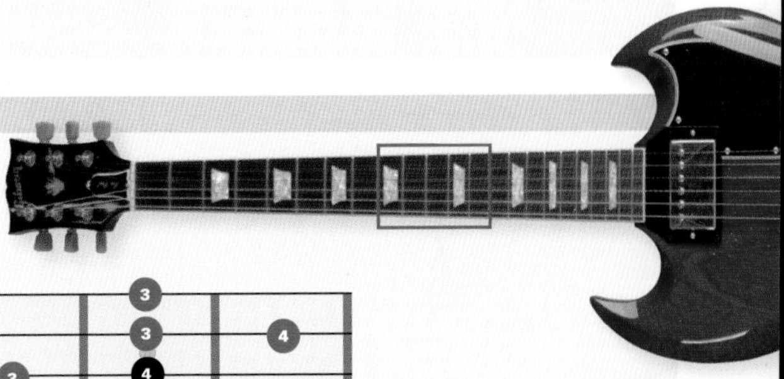

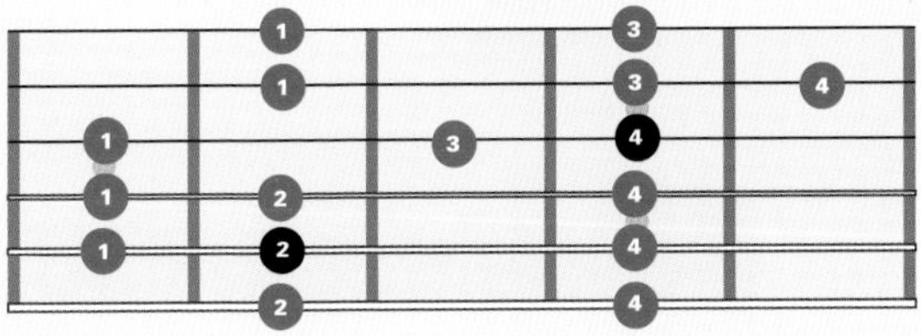

9

SHAPE 5

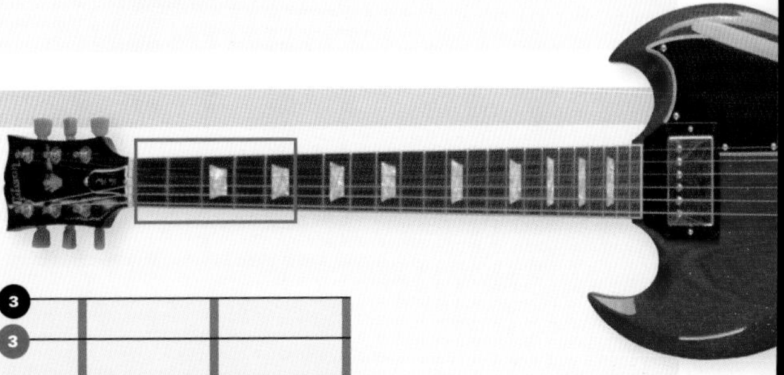

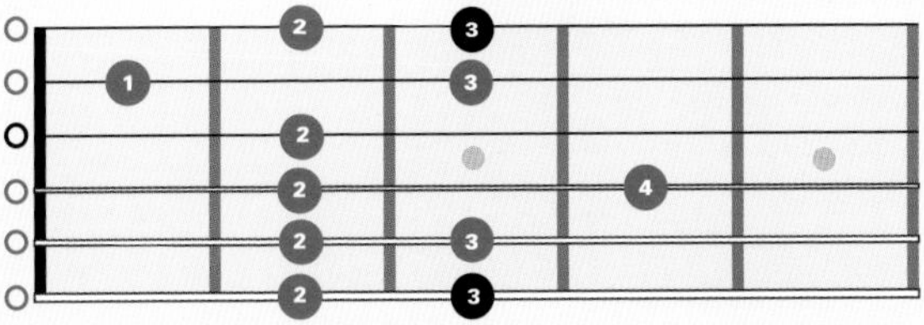

G#/A♭ Major

SHAPE 1

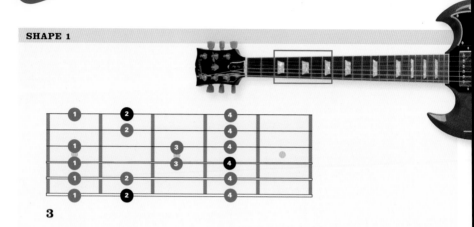

3

SHAPE 2

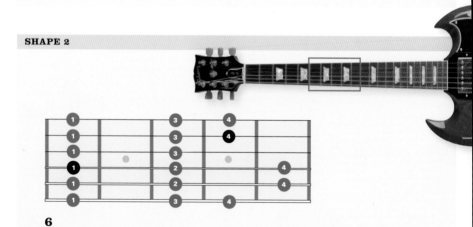

6

SHAPE 3

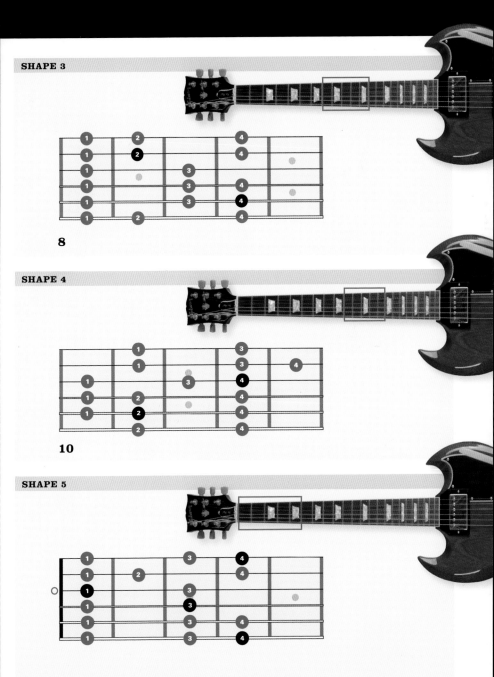

8

SHAPE 4

10

SHAPE 5

SHAPE 1

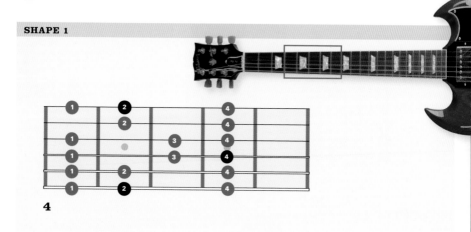

4

SHAPE 2

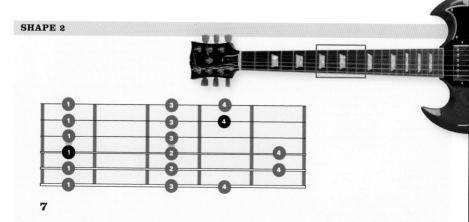

7

SHAPE 3

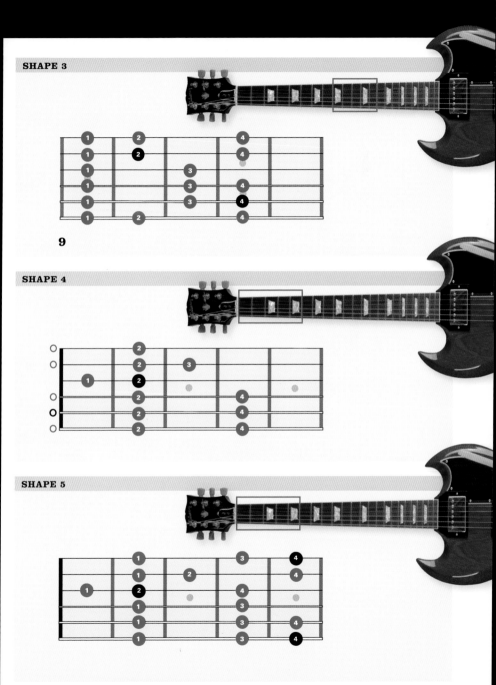

9

SHAPE 4

SHAPE 5

Scale Library

A#/Bb Major

SHAPE 1

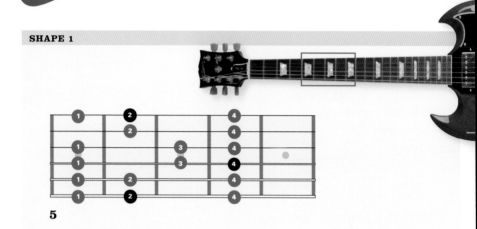

5

SHAPE 2

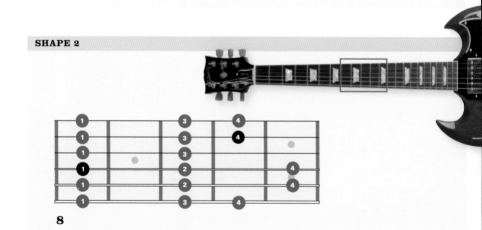

8

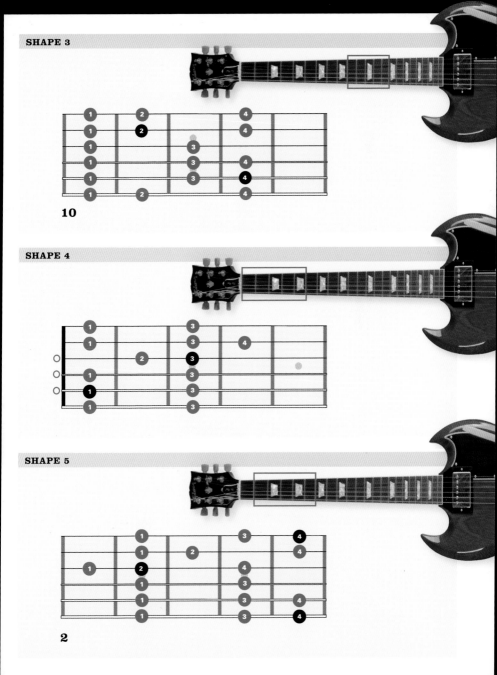

B Major

SHAPE 1

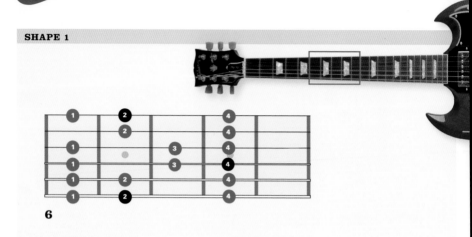

6

SHAPE 2

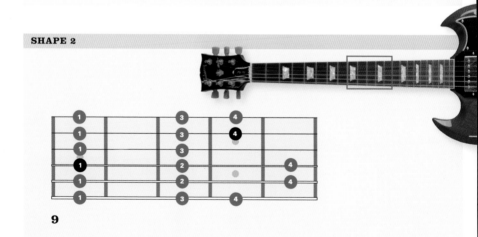

9

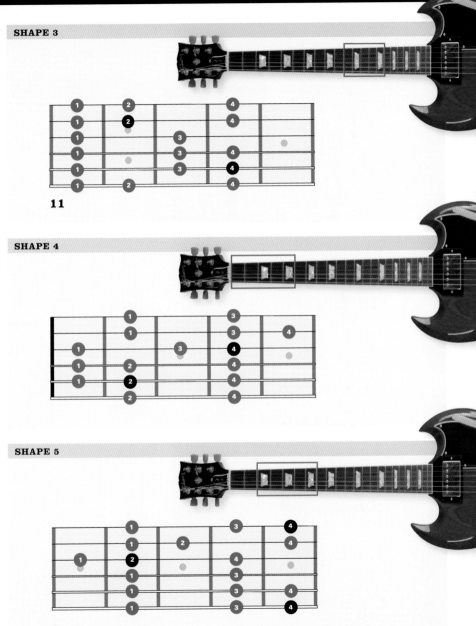

SHAPE 1

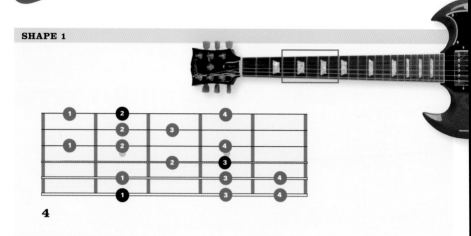

4

SHAPE 2

6

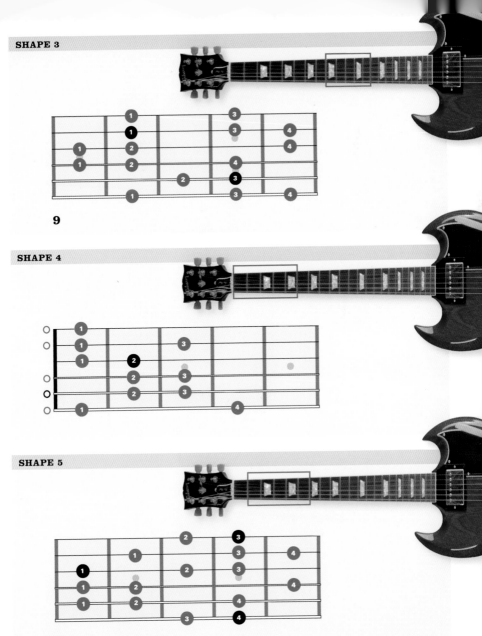

Scale Library

A♯/B♭ Harmonic Minor

SHAPE 1

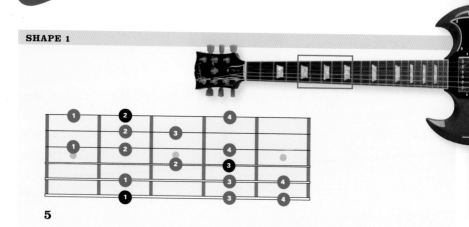

5

SHAPE 2

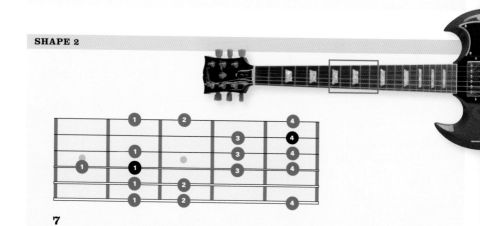

7

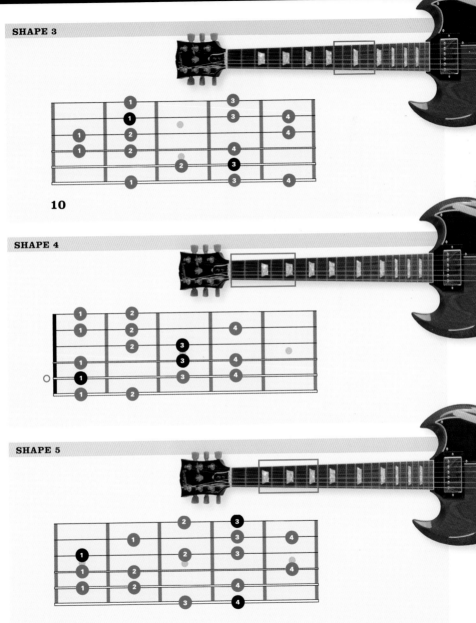

SHAPE 3

10

SHAPE 4

SHAPE 5

3

B Harmonic Minor

SHAPE 1

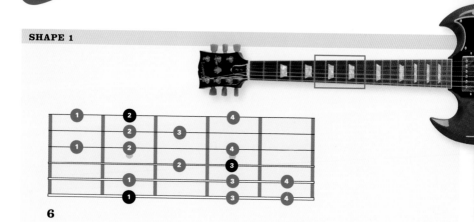

6

SHAPE 2

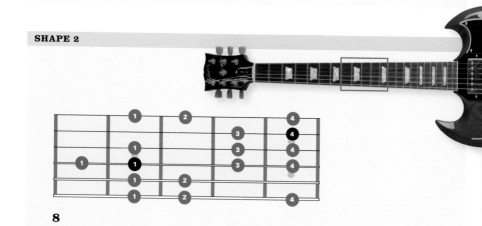

8

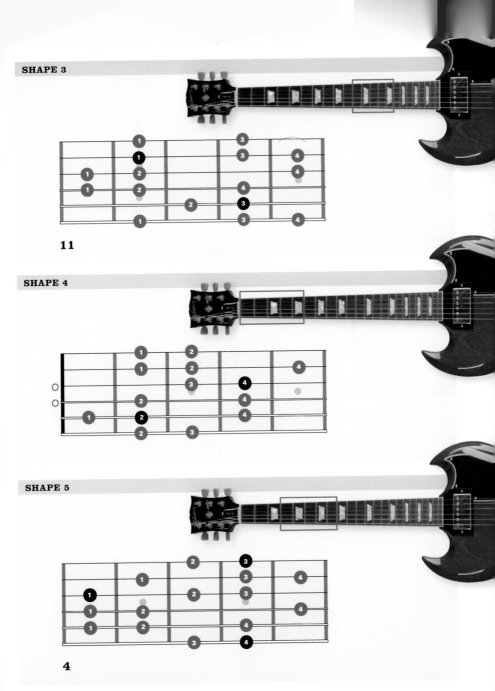

SHAPE 3

11

SHAPE 4

SHAPE 5

4

C Harmonic Minor

SHAPE 1

7

SHAPE 2

9

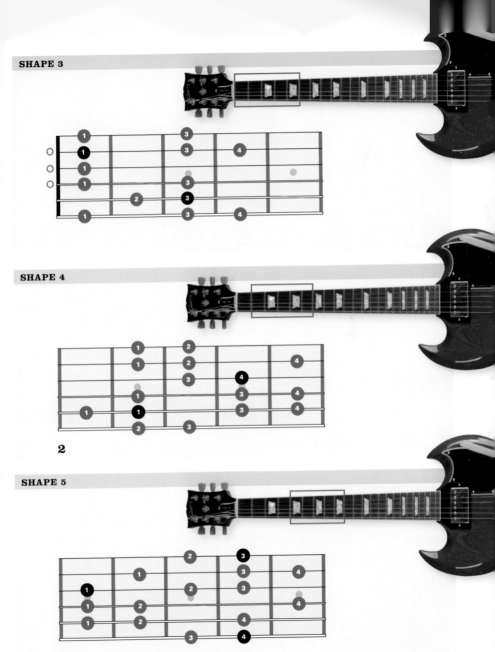

C♯/D♭ Harmonic Minor

SHAPE 1

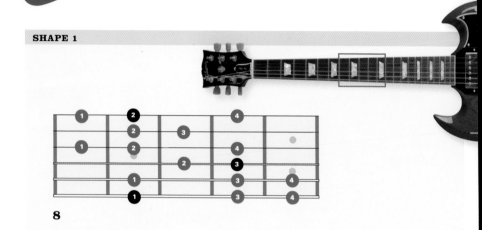

8

SHAPE 2

10

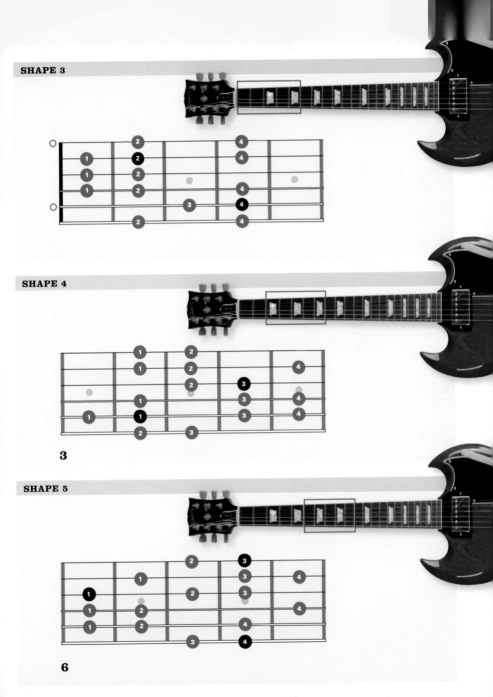

SHAPE 3

SHAPE 4

3

SHAPE 5

6

D Harmonic Minor

SHAPE 1

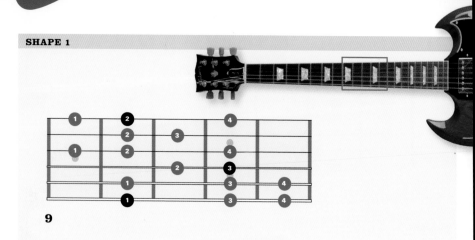

9

SHAPE 2

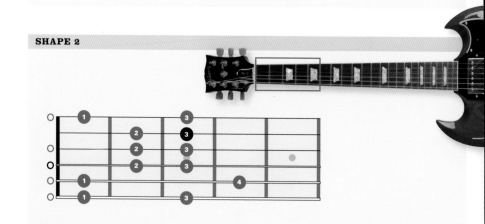

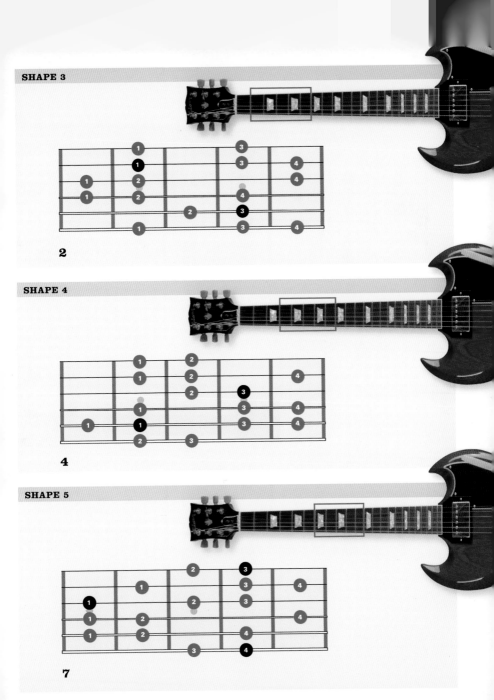

SHAPE 3

2

SHAPE 4

4

SHAPE 5

7

D#/Eb Harmonic Minor

SHAPE 1

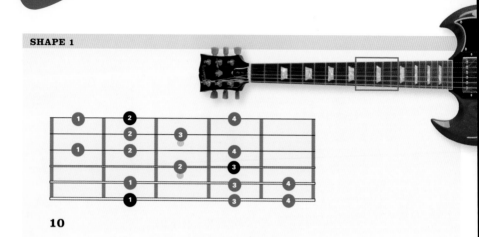

10

SHAPE 2

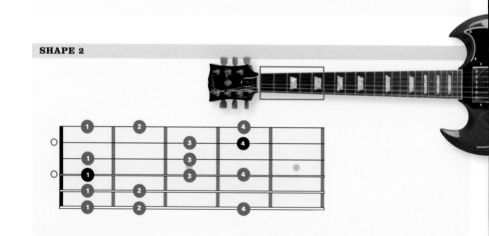

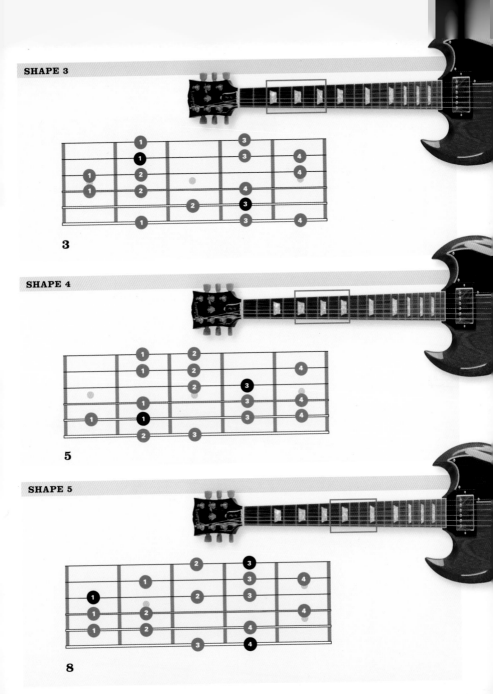

SHAPE 3

3

SHAPE 4

5

SHAPE 5

8

E Harmonic Minor

SHAPE 1

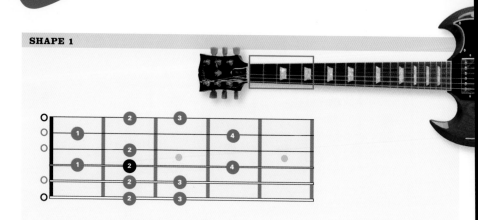

SHAPE 2

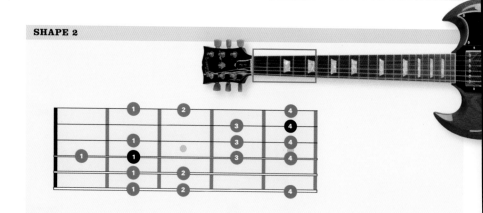

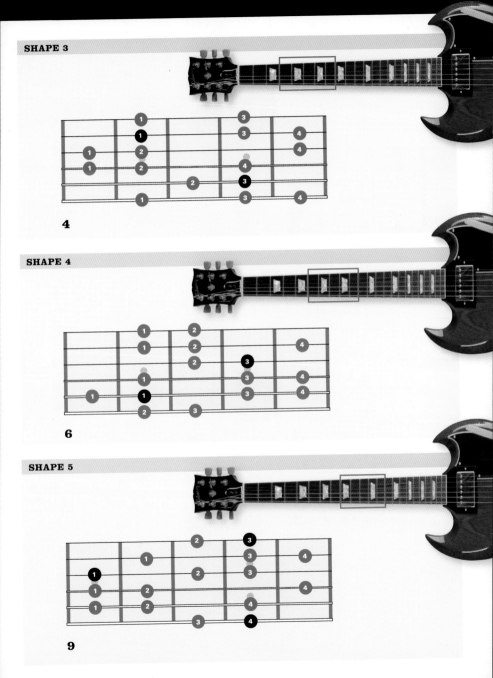

SHAPE 3

4

SHAPE 4

6

SHAPE 5

9

Scale Library

F Harmonic Minor

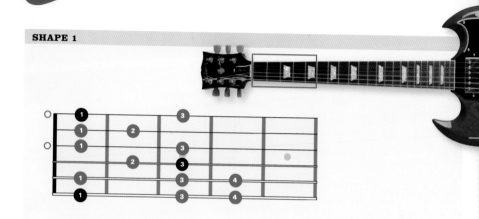

2

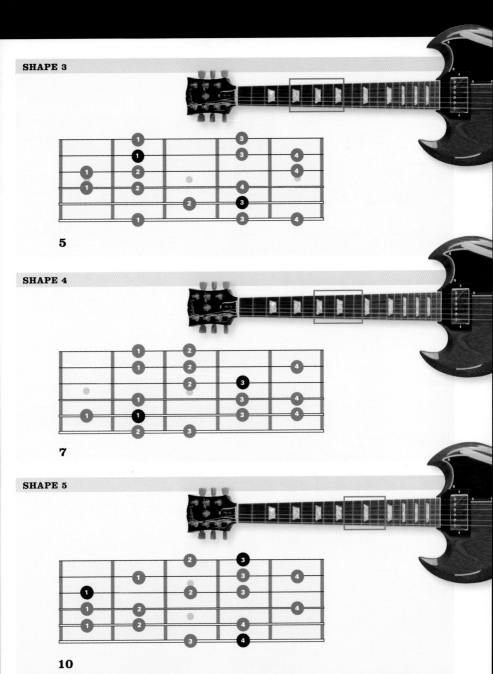

SHAPE 3

5

SHAPE 4

7

SHAPE 5

10

SHAPE 1

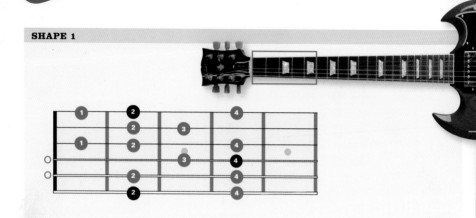

SHAPE 2

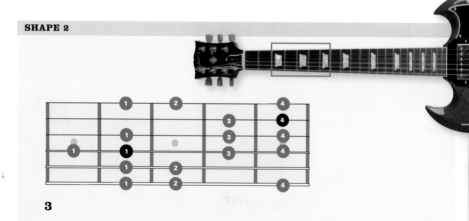

3

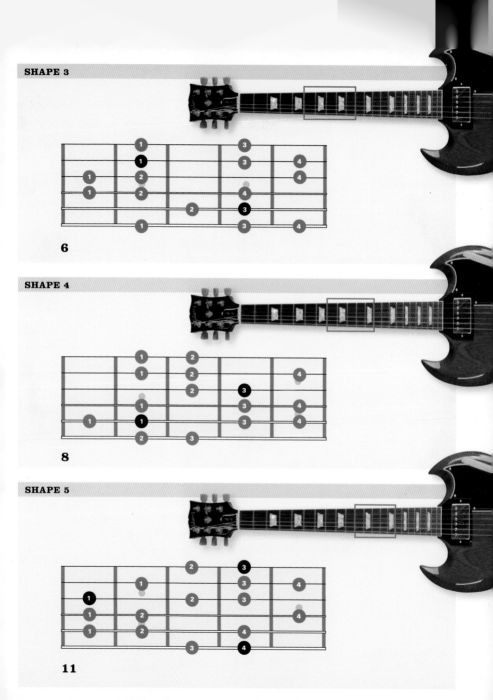

SHAPE 3

6

SHAPE 4

8

SHAPE 5

11

G Harmonic Minor

SHAPE 1

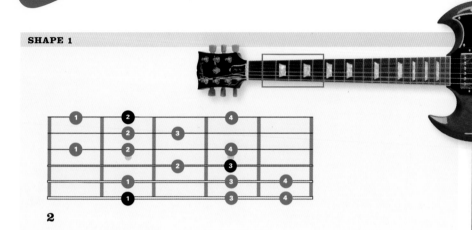

2

SHAPE 2

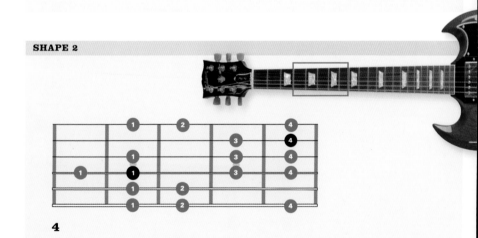

4

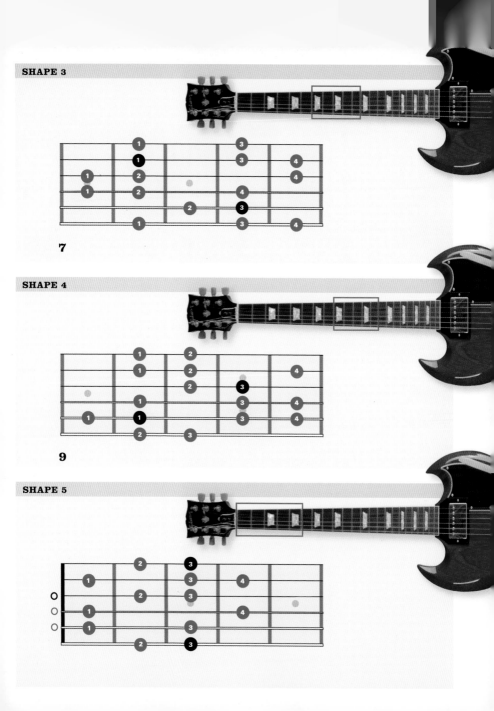

SHAPE 3

7

SHAPE 4

9

SHAPE 5

G#/Ab Harmonic Minor

SHAPE 1

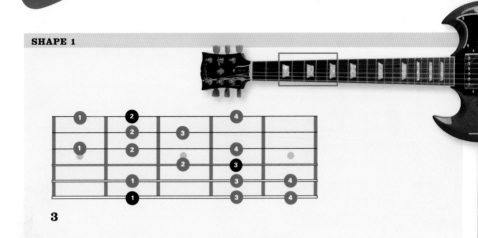

SHAPE 2

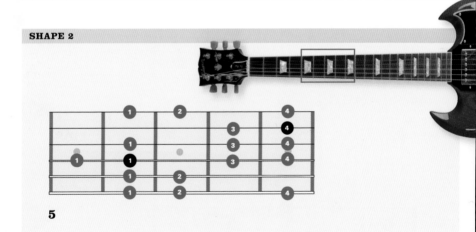

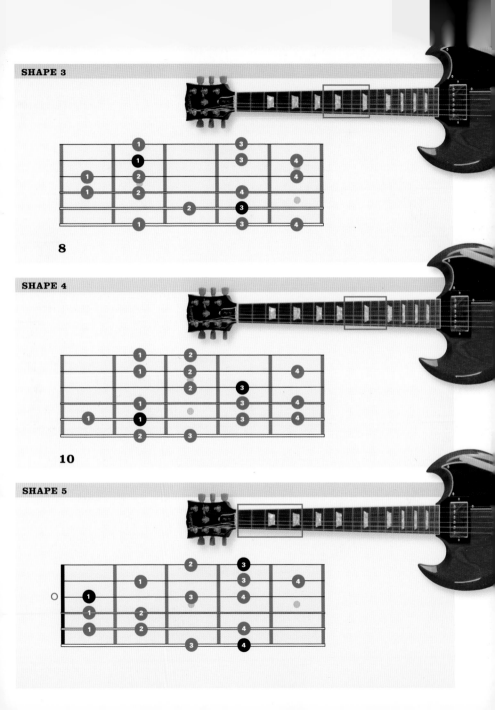

SHAPE 3

8

SHAPE 4

10

SHAPE 5

Index

Credits
Quarto would like to thank the following agencies and
manufacturers for supplying images for inclusion in this book:

Keawchookul, Warin, Shutterstock.com, p.2
Digital Storm, Shutterstock.com, pp.4-5, 10,
Barbol, Shutterstock.com, p.1
Hunton, Philip, Shutterstock.com, p.88
Elnur, Shutterstock.com, p.115

All step-by-step and other images are the copyright of Quarto
Publishing plc. While every effort has been made to credit
contributors, Quarto would like to apologize should there have
been any omissions or errors - and would be pleased to make the
appropriate correction for future editions of the book.

More About the Author
You can find out more about Phil on his website: **philcapone.com**